THE EASY BIRD GUIDE

Eastern Region

A Quick Identification Guide for All Birders

John Bull, Edith Bull, and Gerald Gold
Illustrated by Pieter D. Prall

FALCONGUIDES ®

GUILFORD, CONNECTICUT
HELENA, MONTANA

AN IMPRINT OF THE GLOBE PEQUOT PRESS

Falcon and FalconGuide are registered trademarks of Morris Book Publishing, LLC.
Map by M.A. Dubé © 2006 Morris Book Publishing, LLC.

Library of Congress Cataloging-in-Publication Data
Bull, John L.
    The easy bird guide. Eastern region: a quick identification guide for all birders /
by John Bull, Edith Bull, and Gerald Gold; illustrated by Pieter D. Prall.—
    1st ed. p. cm.
ISBN 978-0-7627-3741-3
1. Birds—United States—Identification. 2. Birds—East (U.S.)—Identification. 3.
Birds—Middle West—Identification. 4. Birds—Canada, Eastern—Identification. I.
Bull, Edith. II. Gold, Gerald. III. Prall, Pieter D. IV. Title.
    QL682.B85 2006
    598.0974—dc22

                                                            2005027247

Printed in China
First Globe Pequot Edition/Second Printing

To buy books in quantity for corporate use
or incentives, call **(800) 962–0973**
or e-mail **premiums@GlobePequot.com.**

Acknowledgments

This book is the product of our collective years of working, teaching, and volunteering at major natural history museums and nature organizations; of leading field trips and lecturing about birds; and of writing about birds for professionals, the media, and the public. We realized that the beginning birder needed easy-to-understand information about birding. The result is this book, which aims to help the uninitiated learn about birds quickly and easily, and to serve as a teaching tool for beginning bird-watchers.

When we conceived the idea of our book, which was originally published as a Macmillan Field Guide in 1985, we wrote it for baby-boomers during the mass exodus of educated and environmentally-aware people from the cities and suburbia to the countryside in the mid- to late 1980s. Today we envision those weathering baby-boomers using this new edition to teach their grandchildren about birds during the 2000s.

There are several people we would like to thank for their suggestions and contributions. Guy Tudor and John Yrizarry offered many helpful ideas about the comparative plates in the illustrated section of this book. The staff at the Department of Ornithology at the American Museum of Natural History provided assistance and access to collections that was invaluable to this work. Thanks go to Laura Strom and Jan Cronan of The Globe Pequot Press for their enthusiastic support of this project. We will also not forget the unswerving dedication exhibited by Lori Andiman as she contributed valuable time and effort, bringing this book back into publication. Pieter Prall would like to thank his late parents, William and Elsie Prall, and his family and friends, especially W. W. and Dr. Bernard Brennan, for their encouragement.

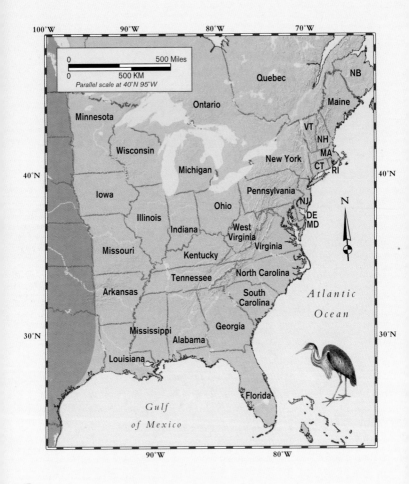

Contents

Introduction 7
   How to Use This Guide 7
   Beginning Birding 8
   Bird Descriptions 10
   Organization of the Plates 11
   Explanation of the Plates 12
Plate Key 14
Identifying Birds by Field Marks 15
   Field Marks 15
   Wing Shapes 16
   Tail Shapes 16
   Bill Shapes 17
   Foot Shapes 18
   Text Descriptions 19
   More Field Marks 20

Bird Plates 22
Blue Birds 22
Red Birds 24
Black Birds 28
Yellow Finches, Orioles 32
Open Country, Grassland Birds 34
Brown Birds 36
Sparrows 40
Large Grayish Birds 44
Small Grayish Birds 46
Vireos 48
Warblers 50
Tree Clingers 58
Woodpeckers 60
Flycatchers 62
Swift, Swallows 64
Nightjars, Hummingbird 66

Cuckoo, Pigeons 68

Game Birds 70

Hawks 72

Woodland Owls 80

Open-Country Owls 82

Geese, Swans 84

Tipping Ducks 86

Diving Ducks 90

Rails, Coot, Gallinules 96

Grebes 98

Guillemot, Loons 100

Cormorants, Anhinga 102

Gannet, Pelicans, Frigatebird 104

White Herons 106

Crane, Dark Herons 108

Dark Herons 110

Stork, Ibises, Spoonbill, Limpkin 112

Shorebirds 114

Gulls 124

Terns 126

Terns 2, Skimmer 128

Further Comments on the Plates 130

Attracting Birds 145

    Feeders 145

    Water 150

    Nest Boxes 150

    Shrubs and Trees 151

Appendix A: Optical Equipment 153

Appendix B: Glossary 154

Index 155

About the Authors and Artist 160

Introduction

This is a book about identifying birds. While it contains much information about other things concerned with birds, its purpose is to help you identify them. It is a quick guide in two senses: First, it provides an introduction to the world of birding, with a general discussion of the hows and whys of the hobby. Second, it is a tool for use on those occasions when you want to identify a bird at your window, in the park, on a walk in the woods, at the seashore, or at a roadside stop during a drive. While the various chapters discuss the pleasures of birding, some bird habits, and ways of attracting birds, most of the information is given to make identification easy.

How to Use This Guide

At the heart of the book are the color plates of birds and the descriptive material facing them. The plates and the descriptions have been designed specifically to enable you to identify birds quickly, even if they alight for only a moment and then fly off.

There are 253 species illustrated in the 54 plates. They are the birds you are most likely to see in the eastern part of North America, from southern Canada (50° N) to Florida and the Gulf of Mexico and from the Atlantic Coast to Minnesota and easternmost Texas (see map). The western dividing line is based on the western borders of Minnesota, Iowa, Missouri, Arkansas, and Louisiana, plus the upper coast of Texas.

The birds are all reasonably common—some throughout the East, some in specific regions of the East, some only in rather compact areas within a larger section of the East. Although no rare birds are depicted, some are rare in certain parts while being abundant elsewhere. The Boat-tailed Grackle, for example, is abundant in the South, Florida especially, but rare in the North. All the birds are reasonably visible within their habitats in the places where you are likely to encounter them—your suburban yard, a city park, a rural farm, the seashore, a woodland, or along a roadside. Not included are birds rarely seen, even by experts, except when voice identification is possible for a beginner, such as the Whip-poor-will. Birds so difficult to identify that only long experience makes positive identification possible are also omitted. We feel that such parameters are necessary for easy introduction to this most fascinating of hobbies.

Keep this book handy—in the kitchen, where you might look out the window, see a bird alight on the patio, and wonder what it is; in your pocket, purse, or briefcase for those times when you are strolling through the park or walking to work, or along the beach; and in your car for those trips on which keeping an eye on the local birds can add greatly to the fun of a vacation.

It is also an invaluable companion for finding and identifying birds on a purposeful walk through a botanical garden, nature sanctuary, or woods.

First, however, read the entire book and browse through the plates to familiarize yourself with the general information and with the overall appearance of various birds.

Beginning Birding

The easiest way to begin birding is to look out of your window. If you live in the suburbs, you know that there are always birds around, even if you haven't been able to identify them. In the city, you have certainly seen pigeons, European Starlings, and House Sparrows.

At a major museum like the American Museum of Natural History in New York, with a large ornithology department, hundreds of bewildered phone callers, letter writers, and visitors seek identification each year of such common birds as the Blue Jay and American Robin, and even of that "strange little brown bird with the big black patch on its throat and breast." In the last case, of course, someone has just noticed for the first time an identifying characteristic of the male House Sparrow, even though that person may have been seeing it every day of his or her life.

Humans have the urge to name things; we feel that somehow we have gotten a grasp on reality or have penetrated to the essence of a thing if we can attach a name to it. One of the satisfactions of birding is being able to name the birds we see, thereby establishing some kind of mastery over the natural wonders that surround us, even in the densest urban locality.

At this point many an urban dweller will scoff and say, "I can spot a pigeon, and that's all there is in my neighborhood." However, that same neighborhood undoubtedly harbors many other species at one time or another, for every bush, tree, or plant and every patch of water (even a muddy rain puddle) is a magnet for birds, which have an uncanny ability to find an oasis in the midst of the dreariest urban desert. For example, in the early 1990s a Red-tailed Hawk nicknamed Pale Male took up residence on the ledge of a Fifth Avenue high-rise in Manhattan. The birds you find depend in large part on your wanting to look and on knowing what to look for. It is our hope that this guide will lead you to observe a little more carefully and to become a little more curious about what you see. You'll find that your neighborhood suddenly becomes a more interesting place.

In the suburbs and in rural areas, awareness of birds is generally more widespread, if for no other reason than that birds have less competition from people, buildings, cars, and noise, so they are easier to see and hear. But repeatedly, people ask for confirmation that the noisy blue visitor to the yard is a Bluebird—"You know, all blue and white with a crest on its head and making a loud racket."

"Blue *Jay*," we say, stressing the "jay."

"Oh," is the usual response. "Is there a difference?"

Indeed there is, not the least being that the Blue Jay is ubiquitous and plentiful, while the increasingly rare Bluebird has nearly been eliminated in some places.

It's not hard to become a reasonably perceptive birder. Start by identifying those birds you see repeatedly around your home. Learn without any possibility of doubt to recognize the House Sparrow, Northern Cardinal, or Mourning Dove. Once you've mastered these birds—and it won't take long—your eye and brain will be sure to recognize that something that flew by was *not* one of those. There lies the beginning of the road to advanced birding, and, one hopes, the urge to wander farther afield—to the pond, marsh, wooded estate, beach, lake, or sanctuary.

Without being exhaustive or exhausting, this guide will also tell you what *not* to look for and where and when *not* to look for it, for the process of elimination is an important factor in identification. Although in birding, as in most activities, there are exceptions to every rule, you don't really have to worry about the exceptions.

The "not" factor is important in eliminating things you don't have to worry about. To give just one far-fetched example, remember the Ancient Mariner and his albatross? Why an albatross?

Because he was a seaman, and albatrosses are found only over the oceans. Therefore, a big bird sitting in a tree in your yard will definitely not be an albatross. You can, with impunity, rule that out, without knowing anything else about the bird in your tree.

The elimination process also operates by seasons. Many birds are migratory and spend various seasons in various places. Thus, flycatchers, vireos, and warblers, which are insect-eating birds, will not be found in the northern latitudes in winter, for there is no food for them.

Bird Descriptions

The descriptions facing each plate, besides giving the primary field marks for each bird, include the bird's habitat and the seasons you can expect to see it, as well as the general range in which it normally occurs. There are two ways to use this information. You can locate a field, woodland, or swamp, for example, and then look for birds that are known to frequent these areas. Experienced birders often operate this way, looking for a specific bird known to inhabit such places at given times. For most of us, however, the more natural way to use this information is to check the habitat and season information in order to confirm or reject an identification.

For example:

You are walking along the windswept boardwalk in Atlantic City, New Jersey, in February. You spot a grayish white bird flying over the beach. You see only the general shape and color. With just that bit of information, you can guess that it's probably a gull or tern; then you can rule out the tern because terns are not found that far north in February—information you'll get from the plate descriptions. Other eliminations are possible, involving size and habitat, for example. The data opposite the plates will allow you to make these.

In the description and discussion of each bird, you'll also frequently find out about some of its distinctive habits and its appearance—not because this is an encyclopedia of bird behavior, but because behavior is often a way of identifying birds. Some birds, for example, are usually seen as they creep down a tree trunk; others almost always climb up. Some birds hop, others walk, others waddle. Some birds fly arrowstraight; others dip and rise as they fly. Where these characteristics are distinctive enough to be considered field marks, they are included in the description.

For example:

After identifying an American Robin by its rust-colored breast, you'll notice that you almost always see it on an open lawn. Then you'll notice that it usually takes a few hops, stops, cocks its head as if looking for earthworms or grubs, and then hops on, occasionally jabbing its bill into the ground to snare a worm. After watching that behavior a number of times, you will be able to identify a Robin from the back without seeing its red breast.

Sometimes you will find in the text such descriptions as "only," "largest," or "smallest." Unless otherwise specified, these wide-ranging adjectives are meant to apply to the bird life commonly found in eastern North America. For example, though we talk of the American Crow as the largest perching bird, the closely related Northern Raven is considerably larger; however, since the Raven is seldom seen in eastern North America, it is not included in the book.

Following the name of each bird opposite its color illustrative plate is the measurement in inches, from bill tip to tail tip.

Organization of the Plates

The plates are, in some cases, designed to group birds according to their appearance or behavior, even when the birds are not taxonomically related. The fact is that many birds, though widely separated by evolution and scientific differences, often look remarkably alike, especially to the novice.

Since this book is intended to be as easy to use as possible, *usually* only the male of each species is shown—not because of chauvinism, but because in the bird world the males *usually* have the colorful, distinctive plumage that makes the bird most readily identifiable. Often the female of the species can be identified with certainty only when the male is nearby. The same is true of immature birds. Where the females and immatures are not pictured in the plates, verbal descriptions are often given to enable you to try to identify the dull-looking bird you saw near the identifiable one.

For simplicity, relatively few plumages are shown for each bird. In Plate 1, "Blue Birds," for example, of the five species illustrated, only two show both sexes—the Indigo Bunting and the Blue Grosbeak—because the females are different from the males. The males are all blue, the females all brown. Our principle is as follows: Where the sexes are identical, as in the Blue Jay, obviously only one is shown; where the sexes are similar or virtually so, again only one is shown—for instance, the brighter male of the Eastern Bluebird. The duller but otherwise very similar female is mentioned only in the text. In the case of the similar male and female Belted Kingfisher, the female looks like the male, except for an additional breast band of another color.

For the same reasons—simplicity and effectiveness—most birds are shown only in a resting position—in the water, on land, or in a tree or bush—in their usual habitat, *not* in flight. Where the flight pattern is readily usable for identification, it has been included. The Northern Mockingbird, for example, is shown with extended wings as well as perched, for the large white wing patches that are the principal clues to its identification can be seen only in flight or when the bird is engaged in behavior known as wing flashing. For most ducks, however, flight illustrations and descriptions would be counterproductive for a novice, for at a distance most ducks are extremely difficult for beginners to distinguish. On the other hand, most hawks *are* shown in flight, since their underwing patterns, as seen from below, may be their most readily identifiable field marks.

In trying to make bird identification as easy as possible, the descriptions opposite each plate have been pared to the absolute essentials. For that reason, many of the details in the paintings are not mentioned in the descriptive "Field Marks," for the field marks are those characteristics that together distinguish that bird from all others. Thus, when you come to sparrows, you'll find that even though each picture shows a brownish bird, the description doesn't mention that fact, since the brownish look is "sparrow-wide," so to speak, and is not symptomatic of any individual species within the group. Such group identification is the subject of the "Further Comments on the Plate." chapter, which also elaborates on how to distinguish similar birds from one another.

Explanation of the Plates

This guide is unique in the way in which the color plates and the accompanying text are arranged. The birds are grouped according to similarity of color, pattern, behavior, or habitat. We have, for example, Blue Birds, Red Birds, Brown Birds, Warblers, Tree Clingers, Flycatchers, Open Country Grassland Birds, and Shorebirds, to name only a few.

The plates ordinarily show the males at their brightest, most recognizable plumage during spring and summer.

No attempt is made to describe bird songs, but for those few whose call is familiar, that fact is mentioned.

The bird world is divided into two main groups of birds: waterbirds and land birds.

Waterbirds include swans, geese, ducks, and other ducklike birds, generally described as waterfowl. Waterbirds also include such wading birds as herons and egrets. Finally, waterbirds encompass shorebirds such as plovers and sandpipers, gulls and terns.

The land birds take in everything else—the birds we see in woods, field, yards, gardens, parks, farms, villages, and city streets: the hawks, owls, pigeons, sparrows, woodpeckers, warblers, finches, and so on.

Most bird guides follow a strict phylogenetic or evolutionary order in presenting the birds, beginning with the supposedly most primitive birds (the loons and grebes) and ending with the most advanced types (the finches and sparrows). In other words, they start with waterbirds and finish with land birds. In this volume, we reverse the sequence, starting with the more familiar land birds of yard, garden, field, and park, such as blackbirds, sparrows, thrushes, and warblers. We end with the somewhat less familiar aquatic types, such as the ducks, gulls, and herons.

Further, to minimize confusion, this book includes only 253 species, rather than the 600 or so that occur in eastern North America. Consequently, the number of plates has been kept to 54, rather than to the 130 that would be required for all the species recorded in the region.

The plates that follow these chapters can be used without further comments, except one: You do need to know roughly what group of birds you're looking for. Did you spot a duck or a gull? A finch or a warbler? The "Further Comments on the Plates" chapter provides an introduction to these groupings, making it easier to use the plates.

You may say that of course you know the difference between a duck and a gull. Fine, that's a good start. But what about the difference between a duck and a goose? A Bluebird and a Blue Jay? Or a Blue Jay and a kingfisher? Knowing such differences—or at least appreciating the fact that they exist—is the first step to identifying what you see.

For example:

The Belted Kingfisher is always found near water, for it feeds only on small fish; you will not find this bird in the middle of a forest or in a desert or anywhere far from water. It has a very large, shaggy head, which makes it look top-heavy. However, it is possible for the beginner to confuse it with the Blue Jay, because both birds have a generally blue-white appearance and both have crests. But the Blue Jay's head does not have that outsized appearance, and the Blue Jay is smaller than the Kingfisher. Further, the Kingfisher dives into the water for its food, something the Blue Jay never does.

To take another example—obvious, perhaps, but basic:

Most ducks don't roost in trees; they are usually (although not always) found on the ground or in the water. So, if you saw a rather large bird perched in a tree, the chances are good that it wouldn't be a duck. This is identification by elimination. Identification is made easier by knowing immediately what a bird cannot be. Before you do any birding, we suggest that you read the material, referring to the plates. It will simplify the process of learning to identify birds. There is also much additional information in the "Further Comments on the Plates" chapter.

Plate Key

Descriptions	Plumage Phases	Locations
M. = male	dark phase	c. = central
F. = female	light phase	e. = eastern
imm. = immature	red phase	n. = northern
juv. = juvenile	gray phase	n.e. = northeastern
	white phase	n.w. = northwestern
	blue phase	s. = southern
		s.c. = south-central
	Seasons	s.e. = southeastern
	summer	s.w. = southwestern
	winter	w. = western
		U.S. = United States

Identifying Birds by Field Marks

O n the following pages you will find black-and-white figures describing bird topography, as well as some examples of wings, tails, bills, and feet. These physical features—and others, such as crests and the various patterns and colors—form what are known as field marks. The following summary of the black-and-white illustrations contains an example of each type of anatomical feature and the color plate on which it can be seen, as well as a brief explanation of use. The various tail shapes have aerodynamic functions.

Familiarize yourself with the examples described below and you will find that learning to distinguish the different birds will shortly become a relatively easy and fascinating pastime.

Field Marks (Body Characteristics)

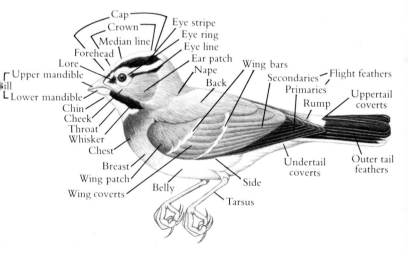

Wing Shapes

POINTED: American Kestrel (Sparrow Hawk), *Plate 29*. Built for speed in the open.

ROUNDED: Ruffed Grouse, *Plate 25*. Adapted for maneuvering through woods and brush.

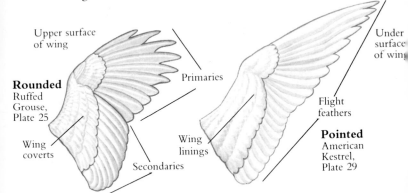

Upper surface of wing

Rounded
Ruffed Grouse, Plate 25

Primaries

Wing coverts

Secondaries

Under surface of wing

Flight feathers

Wing linings

Pointed
American Kestrel, Plate 29

Tail Shapes

FORKED: Barn Swallow, *Plate 22*
NOTCHED: Tree Swallow, *Plate 22*
POINTED: Mourning Dove, *Plate 24*
ROUNDED: Common Grackle, *Plate 4*
FAN: Rock (Dove) Pigeon, *Plate 24*
SQUARE: Cliff Swallow, *Plate 22*

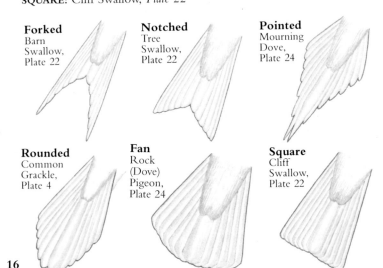

Forked
Barn Swallow, Plate 22

Notched
Tree Swallow, Plate 22

Pointed
Mourning Dove, Plate 24

Rounded
Common Grackle, Plate 4

Fan
Rock (Dove) Pigeon, Plate 24

Square
Cliff Swallow, Plate 22

16

Bill Shapes

PROBELIKE: Common Snipe, *Plate 50.* For probing soft ground.

DECURVED: Glossy Ibis, *Plate 46.* For feeding in water on aquatic organisms, as well as probing in soft ground.

SPEAR: Great Egret, *Plate 43.* For grasping or impaling prey.

SPATULATE: Mallard, *Plate 33.* For straining water to eat animal or plant matter.

HOOKED: Red-tailed Hawk, *Plate 28.* For grasping and tearing flesh.

SHORT, POINTED: Blue Jay, *Plate 1.* A common type of bill on perching birds, for feeding on insects, fruits, and seeds.

CHISEL: Hairy Woodpecker, *Plate 19.* For boring into wood in search of insects.

SHORT, THICK: Rose-breasted Grosbeak, *Plate 3.* For cracking open seeds.

FLOWER PROBE: Ruby-throated Hummingbird, *Plate 23.* For probing flowers to extract nectar while in hovering flight.

THIN, POINTED: Prothonotary Warbler, *Plate 15.* For feeding on small insects.

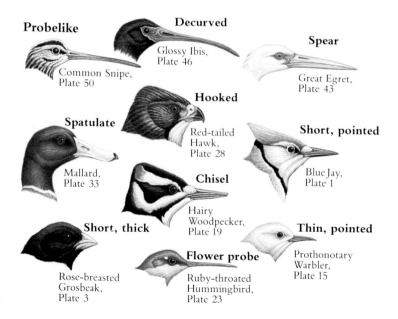

Probelike
Common Snipe, Plate 50

Decurved
Glossy Ibis, Plate 46

Spear
Great Egret, Plate 43

Spatulate
Mallard, Plate 33

Hooked
Red-tailed Hawk, Plate 28

Short, pointed
Blue Jay, Plate 1

Chisel
Hairy Woodpecker, Plate 19

Short, thick
Rose-breasted Grosbeak, Plate 3

Flower probe
Ruby-throated Hummingbird, Plate 23

Thin, pointed
Prothonotary Warbler, Plate 15

Foot Shapes

WEBBED: Black Duck, *Plate 33*. For swimming.

SHARP CLAWED: Red-tailed Hawk, *Plate 28*. For grasping animal prey.

SCRATCHING: Wild Turkey, *Plate 25*. For foraging on the ground.

WADING: Great Blue Heron, *Plate 44*. Long, slender toes give support when walking in marshy areas.

TREE CLIMBING: Downy Woodpecker, *Plate 19*. For gripping bark while ascending trees.

PERCHING: American Robin, *Plate 8*. For perching on twigs, branches, and wires; also for walking or hopping on the ground.

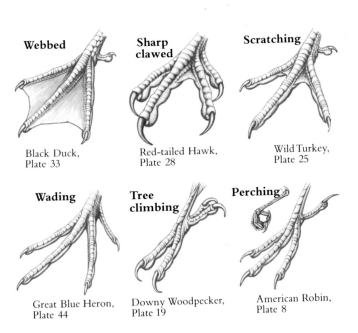

Webbed

Black Duck,
Plate 33

Sharp clawed

Red-tailed Hawk,
Plate 28

Scratching

Wild Turkey,
Plate 25

Wading

Great Blue Heron,
Plate 44

Tree climbing

Downy Woodpecker,
Plate 19

Perching

American Robin,
Plate 8

Text Descriptions

Second in importance to the plates themselves is the description facing each plate. For every bird, using the following four categories of identifiers should enable the reader to identify the bird in question:

1. **Field Marks:** All the important characteristics of size, shape, color, pattern, behavior, and so on that distinguish this bird from all others. No irrelevant or confusing detailed descriptions are included.

2. **Habitat:** Only those places are mentioned in which the bird may be found during the nesting season—usually in spring and summer or, if relevant, in fall and winter. Spring and fall migrations are normally excluded, since birds may occur in many different habitats at those times. However, if the bird in question is found only during spring and/or fall, then the habitats are listed.

3. **Seasons:** It is most important to know *when* a bird is found. If a bird occurs throughout the year, then "all year" is noted. Of course, if a species is found in a certain area during only one or two seasons, then that information will be emphasized.

4. **Range:** It is most important for the observer to know *where* a bird is likely to occur. The map shows the area covered in this volume. For example, a few species live in a very restricted area, such as in southern Florida. At the other extreme, a large percentage of the birds included in this book are widespread in range, and this information is given—for example, "from Canada to Florida and the Gulf of Mexico." It should be stated emphatically that if any bird is restricted in range—say, to southern Canada and the northern United States, or winters entirely south of the States, it goes without saying that it "migrates throughout" our area. Also, in many instances, such as with land birds—especially warblers, which spend the winter in the tropics—*all* of these birds will pass through much of the East during migration, time and again. Finally, it can be assumed that many of our land birds, in particular, are found over most of the region (states and provinces) at some time of year and that only those places on the map are included within the range.

More Field Marks

Band ① Subterminal
    ② Terminal
Red-tailed Hawk, Plate 28

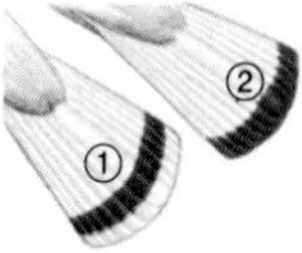

Barred
Barred Owl, Plate 30

Belt
Belted Kingfisher, Plate 1

Breast spot
Tree Sparrow, Plate 11

Cap
Black-capped Chickadee, Plate 13

Collar
Belted Kingfisher, Plate 1

Crest
Tufted Titmouse, Plate 13

Ear patch
Golden-winged Warbler, Plate 17

Ear tuft
Horned Lark, Plate 7

Eye line
Red-breasted Nuthatch, Plate 19

Eye ring
Ruby-crowned Kinglet, Plate 13

Eye stripe
Carolina Wren, Plate 8

Facial disk
Barn Owl, Plate 31

Forehead
Cliff Swallow, Plate 22

Frontal shield
Common Moorhen (Common Gallinule), Plate 38

Hood
Hooded Warbler, Plate 15

More Field Marks

Lore
White-throated Sparrow, Plate 11

Mask
Common Yellowthroat, Plate 15

Median line
White-crowned Sparrow, Plate 11

Nape
Northern Flicker, Plate 20

Necklace
Blue Jay, Plate 1

Neck ring
Mallard, Plate 33

Rump
Yellow-rumped (Myrtle) Warbler,
Plate 17

Serrated
Mergansers, Plate 36

Spectacle
Blue-headed (Solitary) Vireo, Plate 14

Spotted
Spotted Sandpiper, Plate 50

Streaked
Northern Waterthrush, Plate 9

Throat
Black-and-White Warbler,
Plate 19

Throat pouch
Magnificent Frigatebird, Plate 42

Wing bar
Blue-winged Warbler, Plate 15

Whisker
Northern Flicker, Plate 20

Wing patch
Red-winged Blackbird, Plate 5

Plate 1. **BLUE BIRDS**

INDIGO BUNTING 5½"
Field Marks: All blue plumage; female—dull brown above, paler below. **Habitat:** Old fields, pastures, farmland; wooded edges, clearings, roadside bushes, and wires; lawns during migrations; winter feeders in Florida. **Seasons:** Spring, summer, fall; fall, winter, spring in s. Florida. **Range:** Breeds from s. Canada to c. Florida and Gulf of Mexico; winters regularly in s. Florida, often in feeders.

BLUE GROSBEAK 7"
Field Marks: Deep blue; chestnut wing patch and tawny wing bar; heavy bill; female—brown above, buff below; two tawny wing bars. **Habitat:** Roadside thickets and wires, swampy tangles, brushy fields. **Seasons:** Spring, summer, fall. **Range:** From c. U.S. (Missouri) east to s. New Jersey, south to Gulf of Mexico and n. Florida, but common on migration in s. Florida.

EASTERN BLUEBIRD 7"
Field Marks: Bright blue above, reddish below; female—similar but much duller. **Habitat:** Farms, orchards, roadside trees; open woodland, clearings, fence posts and wires in open country. **Seasons:** All year north to edge of winter limits; spring, summer, fall elsewhere. **Range:** Breeds from s. Canada to Florida and Gulf of Mexico; winters north to c. U.S. and along coast to s.e. New York, rarely to Cape Cod. **Note:** Our only hole-nesting thrush—tree cavities and birdhouses.

BLUE JAY 12"
Filed Marks: Bright blue above, grayish white below; crested; black collar; white patches on wings and tail. **Habitat:** Chiefly oak and pine woods; suburban yards and city parks. **Seasons:** All year. **Range:** S. Canada to Florida and Gulf of Mexico. **Note:** Frequents feeders.

BELTED KINGFISHER 13"
Field Marks: Gray-blue and white; bushy crest; heavy spearlike bill; gray-blue breast band; female—very similar, but two breast bands: upper gray-blue, lower rusty. **Habitat:** Lakes, ponds, rivers, streams; marshes, swamps; bays, coasts. **Seasons:** All year in most sections, but rare in winter in extreme north. **Range:** Breeds from Canada to Florida and Gulf of Mexico; winters wherever there is unfrozen water. **Note:** Plunge-dives for fish; hole nester in cliffs and banks.

Plate 1. **BLUE BIRDS**

F.

Indigo Bunting

M.

Blue Grosbeak

M.

F.

Eastern
Bluebird

Blue Jay

M.
Belted
Kingfisher
in dive.

Belted Kingfisher
F.

Plate 2. **RED BIRDS 1**

NORTHERN CARDINAL 8½"

Field Marks: Bright red, including bill; crested; black face; female—similar but light brown; only bill, tip of crest, wings and tail red. **Habitat:** Edges of woods, swampy thickets, hedgerows, gardens; Florida and Gulf of Mexico north to Great Lakes and c. portions of Minnesota and Maine. **Note:** Frequents feeders.

SUMMER TANAGER 7½"

Field Marks: Rose red; pale bill; female—olive green above, yellowish below. **Habitat:** Summer—open pineland, oak woods; migration—towns, parks. **Seasons:** Spring, summer, fall. **Range:** Florida and Gulf of Mexico north to s. Iowa in west and s. New Jersey in east.

SCARLET TANAGER 7"

Field Marks: Brilliant red; black wings and tail; pale bill; female—olive green above, greenish below; fall male—similar to female, but with black wings and tail. **Habitat:** Summer oak forest; mixed deciduous woodland; pine and hemlock woods northward; migration—shade trees in yards and parks. **Seasons:** Spring, summer, fall in most areas; spring, fall in deep south. **Range:** Breeds from s. Canada to Arkansas, Tennessee, n. parts of Alabama and Georgia, and w. Carolinas, but *not* on Atlantic Coast south of Virginia; migrates throughout South.

PAINTED BUNTING 5¼"

Field Marks: Vivid red rump and underparts; purplish blue head; bright yellow-green back; female—bright yellowish green. **Habitat:** Dense thickets and bushes at edges of swamps and rivers; thick plantings along roadsides; gardens, towns, even city parks, as in Charleston, South Carolina. **Seasons:** Spring, summer, fall; winter in s. Florida. **Range:** Breeds in two widely separated areas of South: (1) Texas, Louisiana, Arkansas, s. Missouri, and extreme w. and s. Mississippi; (2) Atlantic Coast from c. Florida to s. North Carolina; winters regularly and locally common in s. Florida, where frequents feeders, often with Indigo Buntings.

Plate 2. **RED BIRDS 1**

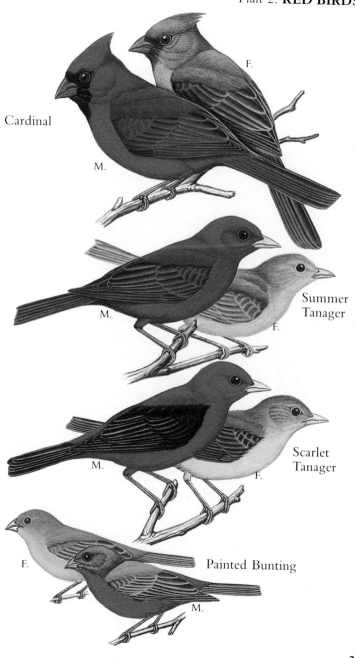

Cardinal

F.

M.

Summer
Tanager

M.

F.

Scarlet
Tanager

M.

F.

Painted Bunting

F.

M.

Plate 3. **RED BIRDS 2**

COMMON REDPOLL 5½"

Field Marks: Red forecrown; black chin; pink breast; heavily streaked above; female—white breast. **Habitat:** Birch and alder thickets; weedy fields, brushy roadsides, and hedgerows. **Seasons:** Highly nomadic; chiefly late winter, more rarely from late fall to early spring. **Range:** Canada to n. U.S., irregularly south to Virginia, Kentucky, and Missouri. **Note:** Frequents feeders.

HOUSE FINCH 5½"

Field Marks: Bright red forehead, eye line, throat, breast, and rump; streaked sides; whitish wing bars; female—heavily streaked brown; no facial pattern. **Habitat:** Ornamental conifers around farms, towns, suburbs, and cities. **Seasons:** All year. **Range:** From n. New England south to c. parts of Georgia and Alabama, and west to w. portions of Illinois, Kentucky, and Tennessee; still in process of spreading outward. **Note:** Frequents feeders.

PURPLE FINCH 6"

Field Marks: Washed with purplish red throughout; unstreaked sides; female—heavily streaked brown, white line behind eye; dark face patches. **Habitat:** Coniferous and mixed woodland; orchards, gardens, and parks. **Seasons:** Spring, summer, fall in Canada; all year in extreme n. U.S.; fall, winter, spring over most of e. U.S. **Range:** Breeds in s. Canada and n. U.S., south to Long Island and in mountains to West Virginia; winters from Canadian—U.S. border south to n. Florida and Gulf of Mexico. **Note:** Frequents feeders.

ROSE-BREASTED GROSBEAK 8"

Field Marks: Red breast patch; black and white pattern; heavy, pale bill; female—heavily streaked brown; white eye line; dark cheek patch. **Habitat:** Moist, open deciduous woodland; groves and orchards; suburban yards and city parks. **Seasons:** Spring, summer, fall in much of North; spring and fall over most of South. **Range:** From s. Canada to Missouri and Illinois in West to Long Island and New Jersey in East, and higher mountains to n. Georgia. Migrates throughout.

Plate 3. **RED BIRDS 2**

Common Redpoll

House Finch

F.

M.

Compare House Finch and
Purple Finch with
sparrows,
Plates 10 and 11.

M.

F.

Purple
Finch

F.

M.

Rose-breasted
Grosbeak

27

COMMON GRACKLE 12"

Field Marks: Black at distance; long, keel- or wedge-shaped tail; yellow eye; close up—iridescent purple, green, deep blue, bronze. **Habitat:** Farms, fields, and golf courses; lawns and parks with conifers; lake and river shores; marshes and wet woodlands. **Seasons:** All year; in n. portions chiefly in spring, summer, fall. **Range:** Canada to Florida and Gulf of Mexico; winters north to s. Great Lakes and c. New England. **Note:** Frequents feeders.

BOAT-TAILED GRACKLE M. 16½", F. 13"

Field Marks: Black at distance; nearly crow sized, but slender and long tailed; close up—iridescent bluish purple; female—smaller, dark brown above, paler below; buffy eye stripe. **Habitat:** Coastal salt marshes and beaches; Florida, also inland; fresh water, fields, farms, and lawns; towns, city parks, as in Miami and Key West. **Seasons:** All year, but migratory in n. parts of range. **Range:** Atlantic and Gulf Coasts from s. New Jersey to e. Louisiana; all Florida.

AMERICAN CROW 19"

Field Marks: Large and chunky; short-tailed; all black. **Habitat:** Farms, fields, woods, parks, towns, and shores. **Seasons:** All year. **Range:** Canada to Florida and Gulf of Mexico.

Plate 4. **BLACK BIRDS 1**

Common Grackle
in flight.

Common Grackle

Boat-tailed
Grackle

M.

F.

American Crow

Plate 5. **BLACK BIRDS 2**

EUROPEAN STARLING 8"

Field Marks: Black at distance; chunky, short-tailed; spring/summer—iridescent green and purple; yellow bill; fall/winter—similar but with white spots; dark bill. **Habitat:** Widespread from large cities to beaches and wooded clearings; also fields, lawns, marshes, shores, and refuse dumps. **Seasons:** All year. **Range:** Throughout. **Note:** Introduced from Europe.

BROWN-HEADED COWBIRD 7"

Field Marks: Glossy black with brown head; stubby finchlike bill; female—all gray. **Habitat:** Farms, fields, lawns, and roadsides; wooded edges and clearings; villages and city parks. **Seasons:** All year; in n. portions chiefly in spring, summer, fall; in s.e. portions in fall, winter, spring. **Range:** S. Canada to Florida and Gulf of Mexico; breeds south to coastal South Carolina and Georgia, but *not* Florida; winters north to s. Great Lakes, c. New England, and s. Nova Scotia. **Note:** Unlike all of our other birds, Cowbirds are parasitic, building no nests of their own, laying eggs in smaller birds' nests. Frequents feeders.

RED-WINGED BLACKBIRD M. 9", F. 7"

Field Marks: Black with bright red shoulder, edged yellowish; female—smaller, brownish, with heavy, dark streaks; light eye stripe. **Habitat:** Marshes, meadows, and hayfields; lightly wooded swamps; coastal scrub; parks and suburbs. **Seasons:** All year; in n. portions chiefly spring, summer, fall. **Range:** Canada to Florida and Gulf of Mexico; winters north to s. Great Lakes and s. New England. **Note:** Frequents feeders.

Plate 5.
BLACK BIRDS 2

European
Starling

winter

summer

M.

Brown-headed
Cowbird

F.

F.

Red-winged Blackbird

M.

Red-winged
Blackbird
in flight.

Plate 6. **YELLOW FINCHES, ORIOLES**

PINE SISKIN 5"

Field Marks: Heavily streaked; slender bill; small yellow patches on wings and tail. **Habitat:** Coniferous and mixed woodland; winter— weedy and shrubby fields. **Seasons:** All year in extreme north; chiefly fall, winter, spring elsewhere. **Range:** Breeds in Canada and n. U.S.; highly nomadic; winters from Canada to c. Florida and Gulf of Mexico, but erratic and irregular in south. **Note:** Frequents feeders.

AMERICAN GOLDFINCH 5"

Field Marks: Bright yellow body; black cap, wings, and tail; female and winter male—mostly dull yellow below, olive above; black wings and tail. **Habitat:** Weedy fields, orchards, gardens, and wood edges; also lawns and city parks. **Seasons:** All year in much of north; fall, winter, spring in Deep South. **Range:** Breeds from s. Canada south to inland portions of Carolinas, west to Arkansas; winters mainly from n. U.S. to Florida and Gulf of Mexico. **Note:** Like the Yellow Warbler, it is often called "wild canary." Frequents feeders.

EVENING GROSBEAK 8"

Field Marks: Golden yellow and dark brown; black wings and tail; large white wing patch; very thick greenish yellow bill; female—dull olive gray; black and white wings and tail. **Habitat:** Coniferous and mixed forest; open woodland; shade trees in rural towns and city parks. **Seasons:** All year in north; fall, winter, spring elsewhere. **Range:** Breeds in s. Canada and n. U.S. from Minnesota to Maine; highly nomadic, wintering irregularly south to s. U.S. **Note:** Frequents feeders.

BALTIMORE (NORTHERN) ORIOLE 7½"

Field Marks: Black and bright orange; female—mainly yellowish; white wing bars. **Habitat:** Open deciduous woodland; tall shade trees, especially elms. **Seasons:** Chiefly spring, summer, fall. **Range:** Breeds from s. Canada to s.e. U.S., but *not* along Gulf Coast or Atlantic Coast south of Maryland; winters uncommonly along both coasts north to Carolinas.

ORCHARD ORIOLE 6½"

Field Marks: Black and chestnut; female and immature male—yellow-green, the latter with black throat. **Habitat:** Shade trees along roadsides, streams, and lakes; orchards, farms, gardens, and parks. **Seasons:** Spring, summer, early fall. **Range:** S. New England west to Minnesota, south to Gulf of Mexico and c. Florida. Migrates throughout.

Plate 6. **YELLOW FINCHES, ORIOLES**

Pine Siskin

American Goldfinch

F.

M.

M.

Evening
Grosbeak

F.

F.

M.

Baltimore (Northern) Oriole

imm. M.

Orchard Oriole
M.

Plate 7. **OPEN COUNTRY, GRASSLAND BIRDS**

AMERICAN (WATER) PIPIT 6½"

Field Marks: Grayish brown above; buffy breast with dark streaks; white outer tail feathers; slender bill; wags tail. **Habitat:** Ground bird of plains and prairies; freshly plowed and burned-over fields, airports and golf courses; lake and river shores; beaches and mud flats. **Seasons:** Fall, winter, spring in South; spring and fall northward. **Range:** Migrates throughout; winters mainly in s. U.S. to Florida and Gulf of Mexico, north along Atlantic Coast to Long Island.

SNOW BUNTING 7"

Field Marks: Chiefly white with black and brown patches. **Habitat:** Ground bird of plains and prairies; also fields, beaches, dunes, shores, airports, and golf courses. **Seasons:** Winter. **Range:** Winters mainly in s. Canada and n. U.S.

HORNED LARK 7½"

Field Marks: Black head and chest patches; white facial pattern; yellowish throat; brown above, whitish below. **Habitat:** Ground bird of plains and prairies; short-grass fields; airports and golf courses; lake and river shores; coastal flats and beaches. **Seasons:** Chiefly winter, but occurs nearly throughout during migration; local in summer. **Range:** Breeds mainly in Canada and n. U.S.; winters south to c. U.S., rarely in southern portions. **Note:** Its name is derived from tiny feather tufts on top of the head.

BOBOLINK 7"

Field Marks: Mainly black; white wing patch, lower back and rump; tawny-buff nape; fall male and female—buff below, dark brown streaks above. **Habitat:** Spring/summer—lush grassy fields and meadows; fall—marshes; rice fields in South. **Seasons:** Spring, summer, fall in North; spring and fall in South **Range:** Breeds from s. Canada to c. U.S.; migrates throughout.

EASTERN MEADOWLARK 9½"

Field Marks: Broad black V on bright yellow breast; mottled brown above; white outer tail feathers. **Habitat:** Grassy fields and meadows; airports and golf courses; winter—coastal salt marshes. **Seasons:** All year, except in extreme North, where occurs spring, summer, fall. **Range:** Breeds from s. Canada to Florida and Gulf of Mexico; winters north to s. Great Lakes and on Atlantic Coast to s. Maine.

Plate 7. **OPEN COUNTRY, GRASSLAND BIRDS**

American (Water) Pipit
winter

Snow Bunting
winter

Horned Lark

Bobolink
F.

M.

Eastern
Meadowlark

Plate 8. **BROWN BIRDS 1**

HOUSE WREN   5"

Field Marks: Brownish above, whitish below; dark bars on wings and tail. **Habitat:** Wooded clearings, rural towns, shrubbery in suburbs, city parks, farms, gardens, orchards. **Seasons:** Spring, summer, fall northward; fall, winter, spring in South. **Range:** Breeds from s. Canada to c. U.S.; winters in s. U.S. from Florida and Gulf of Mexico to coastal Virginia. **Note:** Nests in cavities and nest boxes.

CAROLINA WREN   5¾"

Field Marks: Reddish brown above, tawny below; white eye line. **Habitat:** Brier tangles, swampy thickets, dense undergrowth in ravines and river bottoms; overgrown gardens and farms. **Seasons:** All year. **Range:** From s. portions of New England, New York, and Great Lakes to Florida and Gulf of Mexico. **Note:** Nests in nest boxes and on ledges of wooden sheds and old buildings.

MARSH WREN   5"

Field Marks: Dark brown above, white below; white eye line and back stripes. **Habitat:** Inland—cattail marshes; coastal—giant reed (*Phragmites*). **Seasons:** Chiefly spring, summer, fall northward; fall, winter, spring in South; all year along s. Atlantic and Gulf Coasts. **Range:** Breeds from s. Canada to c. U.S.; also salt marshes from Virginia to Florida and Texas; winters chiefly along coast from Texas to Florida and north to Carolinas, rarely as far as s. New England.

EASTERN (RUFOUS–SIDED) TOWHEE   8"

Field Marks: Black head, breast, and upper parts; rufous sides, white belly; large white patches in tail; close up—red eye, white in southeast; female—similar, but black portions replaced by brown. **Habitat:** Open woods and edges; thick undergrowth; brush fields, thickets, hedgerows; yards and parks with shrubs. **Seasons:** All year, except over much of North, where it occurs in spring, summer, fall. **Range:** Breeds from s. Canada to Florida and Gulf of Mexico, but *not* Texas. Winters north to s. Great Lakes and s. New England. **Note:** This finch is sometimes called "Ground Robin." Towhees scratch vigorously among dead leaves and visit feeders.

AMERICAN ROBIN   10"

Field Marks: Rusty breast; brownish gray back; blackish head and tail; yellow bill; female—similar but paler. **Habitat:** Lawns, golf courses, towns, parks, farms, wooded clearings. **Seasons:** All year throughout much of U.S.; rare to absent in winter in Canada and extreme n. U.S. **Range:** Breeds from Canada to Florida and Gulf of Mexico; winters chiefly in U.S.

Plate 8. **BROWN BIRDS 1**

House Wren

Carolina Wren

Marsh Wren

Eastern (Rufous-sided) Towhee

F.

M.

Compare with Rose-breasted Grosbeak, Plate 3.

American Robin

Plate 9. **BROWN BIRDS 2**

NORTHERN WATERTHRUSH 6"

Field Marks: Brown above; yellowish breast with dark streaks; yellowish stripe over eye; bobs up and down. **Habitat:** Summer—swamps, bogs, moist woods; lake and river shores; migration—along streams and ponds in yards and parks; salt creeks and coastal marshes. **Seasons:** Spring, summer, fall elsewhere. **Range:** Breeds from Canada and n. U.S., south in mountains to West Virginia; winters in s. Florida. Migrates throughout. **Note:** This ground warbler is thrushlike in appearance.

OVENBIRD 6"

Field Marks: Olive-brown above; whitish breast with dark streaks; golden crown bordered with black stripes; white eye ring. **Habitat:** Summer—on or near ground in leafy woods; migration—among thickets and shrubs in parks and yards. **Seasons:** Spring, summer, fall generally, except in Deep South, where mainly fall, winter, spring. **Range:** Breeds from Canada to s. U.S., but not south of n. portions, from Carolinas west to Arkansas; winters along Gulf and Atlantic Coasts from s.e. Georgia, Florida, Louisiana, and Texas. **Note:** This ground warbler is thrushlike in appearance.

HERMIT THRUSH 7"

Field Marks: Brown above with reddish brown tail; white below with dark spots; slowly raises and lowers tail. **Habitat:** Summer—cool, moist, open mixed woods; wooded swamps and bogs; warm and dry pineland on coast of Long Island and New England; migration—city parks and suburban yards. **Seasons:** Spring, summer, fall northward; fall, winter, spring in South. **Range:** Breeds from Canada to n.e. U.S. and in mountains to Tennessee and North Carolina; winters mainly in s. U.S. and Florida and Gulf of Mexico, north along coast, rarely to s. New England.

WOOD THRUSH 8"

Field Marks: Reddish brown head and upper back; white below with heavy round black spots. **Habitat:** Summer—mainly open woodland with undergrowth; rural towns and suburban yards with shade trees and shrubs; migration—city parks. **Seasons:** Spring, summer, fall. **Range:** S. Canada and s.w. Maine to n. Florida and Gulf of Mexico. Migrates throughout.

BROWN THRASHER 11½"

Field Marks: Reddish brown above; white below with dark streaks; long tail; two wing bars; yellow eye. **Habitat:** Thickets, brushy fields, old thorn pastures, parks, and yards with shrubs. **Seasons:** All year in South; spring, summer, fall northward. **Range:** Breeds from s. Canada to Florida and Gulf of Mexico; winters north to c. U.S. and along coast to s. New England.

Plate 9. **BROWN BIRDS 2**

Northern
Waterthrush

Ovenbird

Hermit Thrush

Wood Thrush

Brown Thrasher

Plate 10. **SPARROWS 1**

DARK-EYED JUNCO 6¼"

Field Marks: Slate colored with sharply defined white belly; white outer tail feathers; pinkish bill. **Habitat:** Summer—openings in woodland; migration—weedy fields, roadside thickets, suburban yards, city parks. **Seasons:** Chiefly spring, summer, fall in North; fall, winter, spring over much of area. **Range:** Breeds from Canada and n. U.S. to mountains of n. Georgia; winters to c. Florida and Gulf of Mexico; withdraws in winter from much of Canada. **Note:** Frequents feeders.

HOUSE SPARROW 6"

Field Marks: Large black patch on throat and chest; gray, white, and chestnut head; female—dull, dingy brown; pale eye stripe. **Habitat:** Cities, suburbs, farms, waste areas, refuse dumps. **Seasons:** All year. **Range:** Throughout. **Note:** Frequents feeders.

DICKCISSEL 6¼"

Field Marks: Black patch on yellow breast; chestnut wing patch; gray head; two white face stripes; female—white throat; yellow breast patch. **Habitat:** Grassland, meadows, and hay fields, especially those with alfalfa and clover; prairies. **Seasons:** Spring, summer, fall. **Range:** Chiefly Midwest, locally east to Michigan, Ohio, Kentucky, Tennessee, and n.w. Georgia; rare, but regular in fall along East Coast, but variable in numbers. **Note:** Frequents winter feeders, often with House Sparrows.

SAVANNAH SPARROW 5½"

Field Marks: Heavily streaked; short notched tail; yellowish lores; white crown stripe; pinkish legs. **Habitat:** Grassy fields; meadows, prairies, marsh edges, sand dunes, beaches, lake and river shores. **Seasons:** Mainly spring, summer, fall in North; fall, winter, spring southward. **Range:** Breeds from Canada and n. U.S. south to Missouri and New Jersey; winters from s. Illinois and coastal Massachusetts to Florida and Gulf of Mexico.

SONG SPARROW 6¼"

Field Marks: Heavily streaked; dark spot in center of breast; long rounded tail, often pumped in flight. **Habitat:** Bushes along edges of moist woods, ponds, streams, and swamps; thickets in open fields; shrubs on lawns and in gardens. **Seasons:** All year, but absent in winter in much of Canada and absent in summer in Deep South. **Range:** Breeds from Canada to n. Arkansas and coastal North Carolina; in mountains to n. Georgia and Alabama; winters from s. Great Lakes to c. New England to Florida and Gulf of Mexico. **Note:** Frequents feeders.

FOX SPARROW 7¼"

Field Marks: Rusty red, especially tail; heavily blotched and streaked. **Habitat:** Woodland thickets, undergrowth, hedgerows; brush, shrubs in suburban yards and city parks. **Seasons:** Spring and fall in North; fall, winter, spring in South. **Range:** Winters chiefly in c. and s. U.S., south to n. Florida and Gulf of Mexico, north along coast to Maine. **Note:** Scratches vigorously in leaf litter and frequents feeders.

Plate 10. **SPARROWS 1**

Compare with small grayish birds, Plate 13.

Dark-eyed Junco

F.

M.

House Sparrow

Dickcissel

Savannah Sparrow

Song Sparrow

Fox Sparrow

See more brown-streaked birds, Plates 3, 5–7.

Plate 11. **SPARROWS 2**

TREE SPARROW 6¼"

Field Marks: Rusty cap; dark spot in center of plain breast; two wing bars. **Habitat:** Weedy fields, orchards, gardens, hedgerows; thickets at edges of swamps. **Seasons:** Late fall, winter, early spring. **Range:** Winters from s. Canada to n. parts of Arkansas, Tennessee, and North Carolina. **Note:** The "Winter Chippy" frequents open fields, feeders.

FIELD SPARROW 5"

Field Marks: Reddish cap; white eye ring on gray face; pink bill. **Habitat:** Bushy fields, overgrown pastures; winter—swampy thickets. **Seasons:** All year, except in n. U.S., where it occurs spring, summer, fall; fall, winter, spring in extreme South. **Range:** Breeds in s. Canada, *not* in Texas, s. Louisiana, or Florida; winters from s. Great Lakes and Massachusetts to c. Florida and Gulf of Mexico.

CHIPPING SPARROW 5¼"

Field Marks: Rusty cap; white and black face stripes. **Habitat:** Wooded clearings and edges, orchards, gardens, farms, lawns, especially those with conifers. **Seasons:** Spring, summer, fall in Canada and over most of U.S.; all year throughout much of Deep South; fall, winter, spring along Gulf of Mexico and all Florida. **Range:** Breeds from Canada to Gulf of Mexico, but *not* Texas, Florida, or s.e. Georgia; winters in Deep South and along coast north to s. New Jersey, rarely to Long Island.

SWAMP SPARROW 5¼"

Field Marks: Chestnut cap; white throat; gray breast. **Habitat:** Summer—cattail marshes, swampy thickets, sedgy bogs; migration—weedy fields, gardens, parks with ponds and streams. **Seasons:** Spring, summer, fall in North; fall, winter, spring southward. **Range:** Breeds in Canada and n. U.S. to Missouri and Delaware; winters from s. Great Lakes and Massachusetts to Florida and Gulf of Mexico.

WHITE-THROATED SPARROW 6¾"

Field Marks: White throat; yellow lores; black-and-white or brown and buff head stripes. **Habitat:** Wooded openings, thickets, clearings in mixed woodland; migration—lawns with shrubs in towns and city parks. **Seasons:** Chiefly fall, winter, spring; summer in North. **Range:** Breeds in Canada and n.e. U.S.; winters from n. U.S. to c. Florida and Gulf of Mexico. **Note:** Frequents feeders.

WHITE-CROWNED SPARROW 7"

Field Marks: Black-and-white head stripes; pale gray face, neck, and breast; pink bill. **Habitat:** Thickets and hedgerows adjacent to fields; lawns with plantings. **Seasons:** Chiefly spring and fall; winter mainly in South. **Range:** Migrates throughout, but rare and local along coastal plain from Virginia to Florida; winters chiefly in c. and s. U.S., occasionally north to s. Great Lakes and Long Island. **Note:** Immature—similar to adult but with brown and buff head stripes.

Plate 11. **SPARROWS 2**

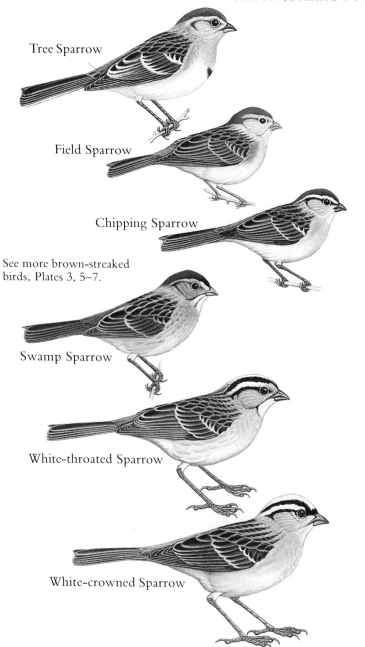

Tree Sparrow

Field Sparrow

Chipping Sparrow

See more brown-streaked
birds, Plates 3, 5–7.

Swamp Sparrow

White-throated Sparrow

White-crowned Sparrow

Plate 12. **LARGE GRAYISH BIRDS**

CEDAR WAXWING 7"

Field Marks: Grayish brown; sleek and crested; black mask and chin; yellow band at tail tip. **Habitat:** Orchards, fruiting trees, vines, and bushes; summer-open woods near water. **Seasons:** Highly nomadic much of year, but all year in much of North; fall, winter, spring southward. **Range:** Canada to Florida and Gulf of Mexico; breeds south to c. U.S. and in mountains to n. Georgia; winters north to s. Canada. **Note:** The red waxlike spots on wings are unique and give this bird its name.

LOGGERHEAD SHRIKE 9"

Field Marks: Black mask, wings, and tail; gray above, white below; hooked bill. **Habitat:** Thornbushes, as in orchards and old pastures; barbed-wire fences. **Seasons:** All year in South; spring, summer, fall elsewhere. **Range:** Breeds from Canada to Florida and Gulf of Mexico, but rare and local over much of Northeast; winters from c. U.S. southward; north along coast to Virginia. **Note:** Shrikes are carnivorous, feeding on insects, more rarely on mice and small birds, all of which are caught and impaled on thorns and barbed wire.

NORTHERN MOCKINGBIRD 10½"

Field Marks: Pale gray above, whitish below; long tail; large white wing and tail patches. **Habitat:** Farms with hedgerows; suburban yards with shrubbery; roadside thickets; utility poles and rooftops. **Seasons:** All year. **Range:** N. U.S. to Florida and Gulf of Mexico; local north to c. Maine and Great Lakes region. **Note:** Derives its name from its practice of mimicking other birds.

GRAY CATBIRD 9"

Field Marks: Dark gray with black cap; chestnut under tail (often obscured). **Habitat:** Shrubbery in parks, yards, and gardens; thick bushes and coastal scrub. **Seasons:** Chiefly spring, summer, fall; winter southward. **Range:** Breeds from s. Canada to s. edge of Gulf states, but *not* Florida; winters in Florida, north along Atlantic Coast to Virginia, rarely to s. New England, and in lower Mississippi Valley. **Note:** Its call sounds like a cat mewing.

Plate 12. **LARGE GRAYISH BIRDS**

Cedar Waxwing

Loggerhead
Shrike

Northern
Mockingbird,
wing flashing.

Northern
Mockingbird

Gray Catbird

Plate 13. **SMALL GRAYISH BIRDS**

BLUE-GRAY GNATCATCHER 4½"

Field Marks: Blue-gray above, whitish below; long black tail with white outer feathers; white eye ring. **Habitat:** Woodland along lakes and rivers; open pineland in South; migration—city parks and suburban yards. **Seasons:** All year in Deep South; spring, summer, fall elsewhere. **Range:** Breeds from s. Great Lakes and c. portions of New York and New England to Florida and Gulf of Mexico; winters along s. Atlantic and Gulf Coasts from North Carolina to Texas; all Florida.

GOLDEN-CROWNED KINGLET 4"

Field Marks: Tiny, short-tailed; black-and-white facial stripes; white wing bars; crown orange (male) or yellow (female); olive above, grayish below. **Habitat:** Summer—conifer forest; migration/winter—mixed and deciduous woods; shrubbery. **Seasons:** Summer in North and in higher mountains; fall, winter, spring elsewhere. **Range:** Breeds from Canada and n. U.S., south in higher mountains to North Carolina and Tennessee; winters south to n. Florida and Gulf of Mexico.

RUBY-CROWNED KINGLET 4¼"

Field Marks: Tiny, short-tailed; white eye ring and wing bars; red crown patch (male only), usually concealed; olive above, grayish below. **Habitat:** Summer—coniferous forest; migration/winter—mixed and deciduous woods; shrubbery. **Seasons:** Spring, summer, fall in North; fall, winter, spring over most of South. **Range:** Breeds from Canada south to n. portions of New England, New York, Michigan, and Minnesota; winters from c. U.S. to Florida and Gulf of Mexico, north to Long Island, rarely inland to Lake Erie.

BLACK-CAPPED CHICKADEE 5¼"

Field Marks: Black cap and throat; white cheeks and underparts; gray back, wings, and tail. **Habitat:** Mixed open woods; alder and willow thickets; shrubs and trees in yards and parks. **Seasons:** All year. **Range:** Canada to c. U.S. **Note:** Nests in tree holes and nest boxes. Frequents feeders, often tame, even feeding from hand. The very similar sibling species, the Carolina Chickadee, replaces the Blackcap in most of South and ranges north to c. U.S.

TUFTED TITMOUSE 6"

Field Marks: Crested; gray above, white below; rusty sides. **Habitat:** Low, wet woodland; suburbs and city parks with large shade trees. **Seasons:** All year. **Range:** C. portions of New Hampshire, Vermont, New York, Michigan, and Wisconsin to Florida and Gulf of Mexico. **Note:** Nests in tree holes and nest boxes. Frequents feeders.

Plate 13. **SMALL GRAYISH BIRDS**

Blue-gray Gnatcatcher

Golden-crowned
Kinglet

Ruby-crowned
Kinglet

See Dark-eyed Junco,
Plate 10 (another small
grayish bird).

Black-capped
Chickadee

Tufted
Titmouse

47

Plate 14. **VIREOS**

WARBLING VIREO 5"

Field Marks: Olive-gray above; whitish eye line and underparts. **Habitat:** Tall elms and maples along roadsides; willows near streams and ponds; aspens and poplar groves; open deciduous woodland. **Seasons:** Spring, summer, fall. **Range:** S. Canada and over much of e. U.S., but rare to absent in s.e. portions from Carolinas to Florida and e. Mississippi and along entire Gulf Coast. Migrates throughout.

RED-EYED VIREO 6"

Field Marks: White eye line bordered by two black stripes; gray crown; olive back, wings and tail; whitish below; red eye at close range. **Habitat:** Deciduous woodland, wooded groves, shade trees. **Seasons:** Spring, summer, fall. **Range:** S. Canada to c. Florida and Gulf of Mexico, but *not* along Texas coast. Migrates throughout.

BLUE-HEADED (SOLITARY) VIREO 5"

Field Marks: White spectacles, throat, and breast; blue-gray head; olive-green back and sides; two wing bars. **Habitat:** Open mixed forest; trees and bushes. **Seasons:** Spring, summer, fall in most areas; fall, winter, spring in Deep South. **Range:** Breeds from Canada south to n. Great Lakes, New York, and c. New England, and in mountains to n. Georgia; winters near Atlantic and Gulf Coasts from North Carolina to Texas and all Florida.

YELLOW-THROATED VIREO 5"

Field Marks: Bright yellow throat and breast; yellow spectacles; two wing bars; white belly. **Habitat:** Deciduous woodland near water; shade trees. **Seasons:** Spring, summer, fall. **Range:** S. Canada, s.w. Maine, and s. Great Lakes to c. Florida and Gulf of Mexico, but *not* along coasts of Louisiana and Texas. Migrates throughout.

WHITE-EYED VIREO 5"

Field Marks: Yellow spectacles and sides; white eye and throat; two wing bars. **Habitat:** Swampy thickets, brier tangles, undergrowth, thick hedgerows. **Seasons:** All year in Deep South; spring, summer fall elsewhere. Breeds from s. Iowa east to Pennsylvania and s.e. New York, south along coast from s. New England to Florida and Gulf of Mexico, but *not* in mountains; winters from coastal South Carolina to Florida and along Gulf Coast of Texas.

Plate 14. **VIREOS**

Warbling
Vireo

Red-eyed
Vireo

Blue-headed
(Solitary)
Vireo

Yellow-throated
Vireo

White-eyed
Vireo

Plate 15. **WARBLERS 1**

PROTHONOTARY WARBLER 5½"

Field Marks: Bright golden-yellow head and underparts; blue-gray wings and tail. **Habitat:** Wooded swamps, streams, ponds. **Seasons:** Spring, summer, fall. **Range:** W. NY and s. Ontario, MI, WI, and MN to Gulf of Mexico; east of mountains from NJ and s.e. PA to c. FL. Migrates throughout. **Note:** Our only hole-nesting warbler; found in tree cavities and birdhouses.

BLUE-WINGED WARBLER 7"

Field Marks: Bright yellow head and underparts; two white bars on blue-gray wings; black line through eye. **Habitat:** Overgrown fields and pastures; thickets along woodland borders and swamps; parks and yards. **Seasons:** Spring, summer, fall. **Range:** S.e. MN and east through s. Great Lakes area to c. New England, south to n. AR, AL, and GA. Migrates throughout.

NASHVILLE WARBLER 4¾"

Field Marks: Gray head; yellow below; white eye ring. **Habitat:** Open mixed woodland; moist thickets; spruce-sphagnum bogs; parks, yards. **Seasons:** Spring, summer, fall. **Range:** Breeds from Canada to n. MN, WI, and MI, east to NY and New England, south to PA, n. NJ and mountains of w. MD; winters along coast of TX. Migrates throughout.

COMMON YELLOWTHROAT 5"

Field Marks: Black mask; yellow throat and breast; female—similar but lacks black mask. **Habitat:** Marshes, moist thickets, bushy pastures and fields; yards, parks, and gardens. **Seasons:** Spring, summer, fall in most areas; all year in Deep South and along s. Atlantic Coast. **Range:** Breeds from Canada to FL and Gulf of Mexico; winters from Deep South and along Atlantic Coast north to MD.

HOODED WARBLER 5¼"

Field Marks: Yellow face encircled by black hood; yellow belly; white tail patches; olive-green above. **Habitat:** Moist deciduous forest with undergrowth; wooded swamps in South; parks, yards, and gardens. **Seasons:** Spring, summer, fall. **Range:** S. CT, NY, and MI south to n. FL and Gulf of Mexico, but *not* coastal TX. Migrates throughout.

WILSON'S WARBLER 5"

Field Marks: Black cap; yellow face and underparts; olive-green above. **Habitat:** Light woodland and thickets, especially along streams, ponds and bogs; gardens, parks, and yards. **Seasons:** Mainly spring and fall; summer northward. **Range:** Breeds in Canada south to c. ME and n. NH; winters on coasts of TX and LA. Migrates throughout.

Plate 15. **WARBLERS 1**

Prothonotary
Warbler

Blue-winged
Warbler

Nashville
Warbler

Common
Yellowthroat

Hooded Warbler

Wilson's Warbler

All warblers are males
unless otherwise noted.

Plate 16. **WARBLERS 2**

YELLOW WARBLER 5"

Field Marks: All yellow, including wing bars; reddish breast streaks. **Habitat:** Willows along streams and swamps; garden shrubs, parks, and yards; coastal thickets; Florida Keys—mangroves. **Seasons:** Spring, summer, fall. **Range:** Canada to GA and n. AR; Atlantic Coast to VA; also Florida Keys. Migrates throughout. **Note:** Called "wild canary."

PINE WARBLER 5¼"

Field Marks: Yellow throat and breast; white wing bars; yellowish line over eye. **Habitat:** Summer—pinelands, taller trees; spring/fall—trees and shrubs. **Seasons:** All year in South; spring, summer, fall northward. **Range:** Breeds from s. Canada, Great Lakes, and c. New England, locally south to FL and Gulf of Mexico; rare Midwest; winters north to AR and Carolinas, and coast to s. NJ.

PALM WARBLER 5¼"

Field Marks: Chestnut cap; yellow line over eye; yellowish below with reddish streaks; wags tail. **Habitat:** Summer—bogs with low shrubs; migration—fields with bushes; yards, gardens. **Seasons:** Spring, summer, fall in North; fall, winter, spring in Deep South; spring, fall remaining areas. **Range:** Breeds in Canada and n. MN, WI, MI, and NH; also n. and e. ME; winters chiefly in s. U.S. from TX to FL, north along coast to VA, more rarely to Long Island.

PRAIRIE WARBLER 5"

Field Marks: Black face stripes and side streaks; yellow wing bars and underparts; wags tail. **Habitat:** Scrub pine-oak; pastures and hillsides with red cedar, sumac, and brier; FL—mangroves. **Seasons:** Spring, summer, fall; all year in FL. **Range:** Breeds locally from MI, s. Ontario, c. NY, and s. New England to FL, west to MO, AR, and LA; winters in c. and s. FL. Migrates throughout.

CAPE MAY WARBLER 5"

Field Marks: Chestnut cheek; yellow below with black streaks; white wing patch; yellow rump. **Habitat:** Summer—spruce-balsam forest; spring/fall—trees and shrubs. **Seasons:** Spring, summer, fall in North; spring, fall elsewhere. **Range:** S. Canada and n. MN, WI, MI, and NY, s.e. to c. VT, NH, and ME. Migrates throughout.

MAGNOLIA WARBLER 5"

Field Marks: Bright yellow below with black streaks; white wing and tail patches; blackish above; yellow rump. **Habitat:** Summer—woods; spring/fall—trees and shrubs. **Seasons:** Spring, summer, fall in North; spring, fall elsewhere. **Range:** Canada south to n. Great Lakes, higher NY, New England, and mountains to VA and WV. Migrates throughout.

CANADA WARBLER 5¼"

Field Marks: Blue-gray above; yellow eye ring and underparts; necklace of black streaks. **Habitat:** Forest undergrowth, thickets, shrubs, parks, and gardens. **Seasons:** Spring, summer, fall in North and higher mtns.; spring, fall elsewhere. **Range:** Canada to n. MN, WI, and MI, east to NY and New England and s. in higher mountains to n. GA; also locally on coast from MA to c. NJ. Migrates throughout.

Plate 16. **WARBLERS 2**

Yellow Warbler

Pine Warbler

Palm Warbler

Prairie Warbler

Cape May Warbler

Magnolia Warbler

Canada Warbler

All warblers are males unless otherwise noted.

Plate 17. **WARBLERS 3**

BLACKPOLL WARBLER 5¼"

Field Marks: Black cap and whiskers; white cheeks; dark above, white below; black streaks; white wing bars. **Habitat:** Summer—spruce balsam forest; migration—shade trees. **Seasons:** Spring, summer, fall in North; spring, fall southward. **Range:** Breeds in c. Canada and coastal Nova Scotia, higher mountains of New England and NY. Migrates throughout.

BLACK-THROATED BLUE WARBLER 5"

Field Marks: Black cheeks. throat, and sides; grayish blue above; white wing patch, breast, and belly. **Habitat:** Forest with undergrowth; clearings. **Seasons:** Spring, summer, fall in North; spring, fall southward. **Range:** Breeds from s. Canada to Great Lakes region from MN to NY and New England, and higher parts to n. GA; winters occasionally in s. FL. Migrates throughout.

YELLOW-THROATED WARBLER 5"

Field Marks: Bright yellow throat and chest; black-and-white face; black streaks on white sides; gray above with white wing bars. **Habitat:** Oak and pine forest; in South also river bottoms and wooded swamps; shade trees on migration. **Seasons:** All year in winter range; otherwise, spring, summer, fall. **Range:** Breeds from MO, IL, IN, OH, and WV to Gulf of Mexico and from s. NJ and DE to c. FL, winters from s.e. LA and east along Gulf, all FL, and to coastal SC.

YELLOW-RUMPED (MYRTLE) WARBLER 5¼"

Field Marks: Yellow rump, crown, and sides; black face and chest; dark gray above; white wing bars, throat, breast, and belly; fall/winter—much duller, brownish above, and whitish below, but with *yellow* rump. **Habitat:** Summer—open forest; spring/fall—shrubs and trees; winter—coastal bayberry thickets. **Seasons:** Chiefly spring, summer, fall in North; fall, winter, spring in South; winter mainly on coast. **Range:** Breeds from Canada to n. Great Lakes, c. New England, and NY, and higher mountains to n.e. PA; winters n. to s. Great Lakes and along coast to Cape Cod, rarely to ME. Migrates throughout.

BLACK-THROATED GREEN WARBLER 5"

Field Marks: Bright yellow face; black throat, chest, and sides; olive-green crown and back; white wing bars. **Habitat:** Summer—conifer forest, less often mixed woodland; cypress swamps in South; migration—trees and bushes. **Seasons:** Spring, summer, fall in North; mainly spring, fall in South. **Range:** Breeds in Canada and n. U.S. and in mountains to n. GA and AL; also coast from s.e. VA to SC; winters rarely in s. FL and TX. Migrates throughout.

GOLDEN-WINGED WARBLER 5"

Field Marks: Black face, throat, and chest; yellow forecrown and wing patch; bluish gray above and whitish below. **Habitat:** Summer—fields and pastures; thickets in clearings; migration—trees and bushes. **Seasons:** Spring, summer, fall in North; spring, fall in South. **Range:** Breeds locally from e. MN, WI, MI, s.e. Ontario, w. and s.e. NY and MA; south at higher parts to n. GA. Migrates throughout.

Plate 17. **WARBLERS 3**

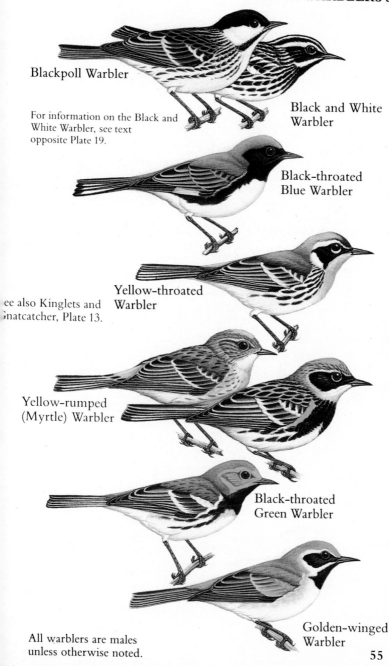

Blackpoll Warbler

For information on the Black and White Warbler, see text opposite Plate 19.

Black and White Warbler

Black-throated Blue Warbler

Yellow-throated Warbler

ee also Kinglets and Gnatcatcher, Plate 13.

Yellow-rumped (Myrtle) Warbler

Black-throated Green Warbler

Golden-winged Warbler

All warblers are males unless otherwise noted.

Plate 18. **WARBLERS 4**

NORTHERN PARULA WARBLER 4½"

Field Marks: Yellow throat and breast separated by dark band; mainly gray-blue above; white wing bar and belly. **Habitat:** Coniferous and deciduous woodland; bogs; river bottoms; in South also cypress swamps; trees and bushes. **Seasons:** Spring, summer, fall; winter in extreme South. **Range:** Breeds from s. Canada south to c. Florida and Gulf of Mexico, but rare and local over much of Midwest; winters in s. Florida and coastal Texas.

CHESTNUT-SIDED WARBLER 5"

Field Marks: Chestnut sides; yellow crown; black-and-white face; light wing bars; white below. **Habitat:** Second-growth woodland; bushy pastures, thickets, trees, and shrubs. **Seasons:** Spring, summer, fall in North; spring, fall in South. **Range:** Breeds from s. Canada to s. Great Lakes and n. U.S. and south in mountains to n. Georgia. Migrates throughout.

BAY-BREASTED WARBLER 5¼"

Field Marks: Chestnut crown, throat, and sides; black forecrown and face; buff neck patch; white wing bars and belly. **Habitat:** Mixed forest; open woodland; shade trees. **Seasons:** Spring, summer, fall in North; spring, fall in South. **Range:** Breeds in s. Canada and n. portions of Minnesota, New York, Vermont, and New Hampshire, s.e. to c. Maine. Migrates throughout.

BLACKBURNIAN WARBLER 5"

Field Marks: Bright orange throat, chest, and head; black cheek patch, side streaks, and upper parts; white wing patch, breast, and belly. **Habitat:** Mixed forest; shade trees. **Seasons:** Spring, summer, fall in North and higher mountains; spring, fall in South. **Range:** Breeds in s. Canada and n. U.S., and south in mountains to n. Georgia. Migrates throughout.

AMERICAN REDSTART 5"

Field Marks: Black head and body; orange wing and tail patches; white belly; female—like male, but with yellow patches; olive above, white below, gray head. **Habitat:** Open woodland clearings; trees and shrubs. **Seasons:** Spring, summer, fall; spring, fall on s. Atlantic and Gulf Coasts. **Range:** Breeds in Canada and nearly throughout e. U.S., but absent from Florida, and the Gulf Coast, and the Atlantic Coast south of Virginia; winters north to s. Florida and along Texas coast. Migrates throughout. **Note:** Redstarts are very active, flitting about, butterfly-like, flashing their bright colors by spreading the tail and drooping their wings.

Plate 18. **WARBLERS 4**

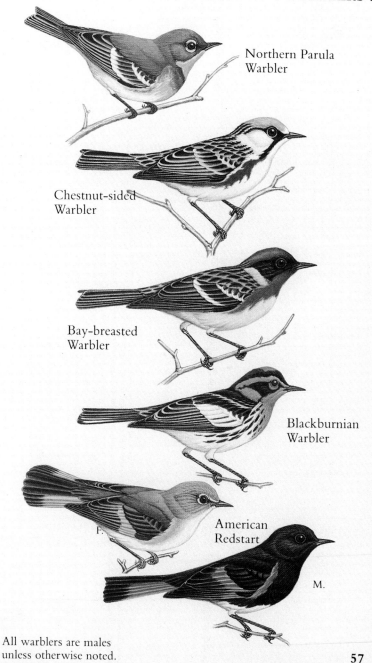

Northern Parula
Warbler

Chestnut-sided
Warbler

Bay-breasted
Warbler

Blackburnian
Warbler

American
Redstart

F.

M.

All warblers are males
unless otherwise noted.

Plate 19. **TREE CLINGERS**

DOWNY WOODPECKER 6½"

Field Marks: Generally black-and-white pattern; white back and underparts; red hindcrown; short bill; female—like male but *no* red. **Habitat:** Open woodland; orchards, shade trees; shrubbery. **Seasons:** All year. **Range:** Canada to Florida and Gulf of Mexico. **Note:** Frequents feeders.

HAIRY WOODPECKER 9½"

Field Marks: Almost identical to Downy Woodpecker, but larger; longer bill. **Habitat:** Forest; shade trees. **Seasons:** All year. **Range:** Canada to Florida and Gulf of Mexico. **Note:** The Hairy Woodpecker is much less common than its small relative and is usually found in thicker woods.

BLACK-AND-WHITE WARBLER 5"

Field Marks: Head and body striped black-and-white; male—black throat; female—white throat. **Habitat:** Woodland; shade trees, thickets, shrubs. **Seasons:** Chiefly spring, summer, fall; fall, winter, spring, in Deep South. **Range:** Breeds from s. Canada to Gulf states, but *not* Florida; winters in s. portions of Gulf states, all of Florida, and north along Atlantic Coast to South Carolina. **Note:** Climbs and creeps along branches and tree trunks. See Blackpoll Warbler for comparison, Plate 17.

BROWN CREEPER 5"

Field Marks: Brown above, white below; slender decurved bill; stiff pointed tail. **Habitat:** Woodland; shade trees, shrubs, thickets. **Seasons:** All year in North, but uncommon in winter; fall, winter, spring southward. **Range:** Breeds in Canada and n. U.S. and in higher mountains to North Carolina and Tennessee; winters from localized spots in n. U.S. to c. Florida and Gulf of Mexico. **Note:** Our only small brown bird that climbs up trees, where it blends in with the bark. Where trees are absent, will ascend poles and posts.

WHITE-BREASTED NUTHATCH 5½"

Field Marks: Blue-gray above, white below; male—black cap; female—gray cap. **Habitat:** Deciduous forest; swampy woodland; shade trees. **Seasons:** All year. **Range:** S. Canada to c. Florida and Gulf of Mexico. **Note:** Nuthatches are our only birds that descend head down. They frequent feeders.

RED-BREASTED NUTHATCH 4½"

Field Marks: Black-and-white striped face; rusty below, blue gray above; male—black cap; female—gray cap. **Habitat:** Summer—conifer forest; winter—chiefly pines; migration—conifers and hardwoods. **Seasons:** All year in North; fall, winter, spring southward. **Range:** Breeds in Canada and n. U.S. and in higher mountains to North Carolina and Tennessee; winters from n. U.S. to n. Florida and Gulf of Mexico; in fall most numerous along Atlantic Coast.

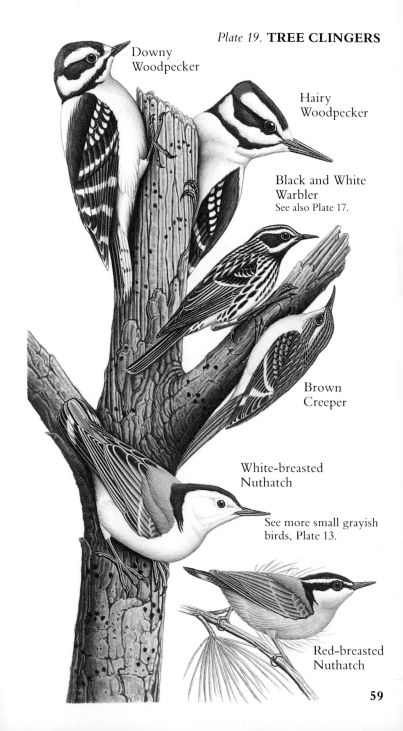

Plate 19. **TREE CLINGERS**

Downy
Woodpecker

Hairy
Woodpecker

Black and White
Warbler
See also Plate 17.

Brown
Creeper

White-breasted
Nuthatch

See more small grayish
birds, Plate 13.

Red-breasted
Nuthatch

Plate 20. **WOODPECKERS**

PILEATED WOODPECKER 18"

Field Marks: Red crest; black-and-white face; black body; female—black forecrown; lacks red whisker. **Habitat:** Forest; light woodland near towns and in parks. **Seasons:** All year. **Range:** Canada to Florida and Gulf of Mexico; most numerous in the South. **Note:** Our largest woodpecker. May visit feeders adjacent to wooded areas. (Ivory-billed is larger but believed near extinction.)

RED-HEADED WOODPECKER 9½"

Field Marks: Red head; white wing patches, rump, and underparts; blue-black back, wings and tail. Immature—brownish; white wing patches. **Habitat:** Groves, farms, orchards, shade trees, wooded swamps, river bottoms. **Seasons:** All year, but rare in winter in North. **Range:** S. Canada to Florida and Gulf of Mexico; rare in New England. **Comment:** Frequents feeders.

YELLOW-BELLIED SAPSUCKER 9"

Field Marks: Long white wing patch; red, black, and white head; yellowish belly; female—white throat; immature—brown head. **Habitat:** Light open woodland, orchards, shade trees. **Seasons:** Spring, summer, fall in North; fall, winter, spring southward. **Range:** Breeds in s. Canada and n. U.S., south in the mountains to West Virginia; winters mainly in c. and s. states.

RED-BELLIED WOODPECKER 10"

Field Marks: Zebra-backed; red cap and nape; whitish face and underparts; female—red nape. **Habitat:** Wet woodland, river bottoms, groves, orchards, towns. **Seasons:** All year. **Range:** S. Great Lakes area to Florida and Gulf of Mexico; north along Atlantic Coast to s. Connecticut; most numerous in the South. **Note:** This bird is misnamed; it does *not* have red belly, only slight trace of red on vent. Frequents feeders.

NORTHERN FLICKER 13"

Field Marks: Brown back with black bars; spotted below; black and tan face; yellow wing linings; white rump. **Habitat:** Open woodland, farms, shade trees, lawns. **Seasons:** Chiefly spring, summer, fall in North; all year in South. **Range:** Canada to Florida and Gulf of Mexico. **Note:** Often feeds on ground.

Plate 20.
WOODPECKERS

Pileated Woodpecker M.

F. in flight.

Red-headed Woodpecker

adult

imm.

Yellow-bellied Sapsucker

Red-bellied Woodpecker

M.

F.

Northern Flicker

Plate 21. **FLYCATCHERS**

GRAY KINGBIRD 9"

Field Marks: Gray above, white below; heavy bill; dark ear patch; notched tail. **Habitat:** Mangroves, scattered trees; roadside wires; city parks, as in Miami and Key West. **Seasons:** Spring, summer, fall. **Range:** Gulf and Atlantic coasts of Florida; rarely north to South Carolina and west to Alabama and Mississippi.

EASTERN KINGBIRD 8"

Field Marks: Black above, white below; broad white band at end of tail. **Habitat:** Farms, orchards, roadsides, lake and river shores; fence posts; utility wires. **Seasons:** Spring, summer, fall. **Range:** S. Canada to Florida and Gulf of Mexico.

EASTERN PHOEBE 7"

Field Marks: Drab; dark above, light below; wags tail. **Habitat:** Nesting—woodland clearings; migration—suburban yards, city parks. **Seasons:** Chiefly spring, summer, fall in North; all year in much of South. **Range:** Breeds from Canada to s. U.S., except Florida; winters in Florida, north to the Carolinas, Tennessee, and Arkansas, west to Texas; rarely as far north as coastal Maryland. **Note:** Nests under bridges, ledges of barns, porches of country houses.

EASTERN WOOD-PEWEE 6½"

Field Marks: Drab; dark above, light below; two wing bars. **Habitat:** Woodlands, orchards, shade trees. **Seasons:** Spring, summer, fall. **Range:** S. Canada to n. Florida and Gulf of Mexico. Migrates throughout.

GREAT CRESTED FLYCATCHER 8½"

Field Marks: Gray throat and breast; yellow belly; rufous patches in wings and tail; olive-brown head and neck. **Habitat:** Woodland, orchards, shade trees. **Seasons:** Spring, summer, fall. **Range:** S. Canada to Florida and Gulf of Mexico; winters rarely in s. Florida. **Note:** Nests in tree cavities, nest boxes, and on fence posts and utility posts.

LEAST FLYCATCHER 5¼"

Field Marks: Dark above, light below; eye ring; two wing bars. **Habitat:** Shade trees, farms, orchards, groves, open woodland. **Seasons:** Spring, summer, fall. **Range:** Breeds from Canada to Iowa and Pennsylvania; south in the mountains to n. Georgia; migrates throughout the South. **Note:** Our smallest flycatcher.

Plate 21. **FLYCATCHERS**

Gray
Kingbird

Eastern
Kingbird

Eastern
Phoebe

Great
Crested
Flycatcher

Eastern
Wood-Pewee

Least
Flycatcher

63

Plate 22. **SWIFT, SWALLOWS**

CHIMNEY SWIFT 5½"

Field Marks: Dark sooty-brown; long, curved, pointed wings. **Habitat:** Open sky—always seen on the wing, except when entering or leaving chimneys. **Seasons:** Spring, summer, fall. **Range:** S. Canada to Florida and Gulf of Mexico. **Note:** Nests and roosts in chimneys.

BANK SWALLOW 5"

Field Marks: Dark brown above; brown chest band on white underparts. **Habitat:** Open country over land and water. **Seasons:** Spring, summer, early fall in North; chiefly spring, fall in South. **Range:** Canada to Florida and Gulf of Mexico, but in southern states only during migration. **Note:** Nests in holes in sand and gravel banks.

TREE SWALLOW 6"

Field Marks: Glossy blue-green above, white below. **Habitat:** Open country near water; marshes and meadows; wooded swamps, especially those with dead trees. **Seasons:** Spring, summer, fall in North; fall, winter, spring southward. **Range:** Breeds in Canada and n. U.S.; winters along Atlantic Coast from Virginia to Georgia and all of Florida; also along Gulf Coast from Alabama to Texas. **Note:** Nests in tree holes and nest boxes.

BARN SWALLOW 7"

Field Marks: Deeply forked tail; deep blue above; chestnut throat; cinnamon breast and belly. **Habitat:** Farms, fields, marshes, ponds. **Seasons:** Spring, summer, fall. **Range:** Breeds from s. Canada to s.e. U.S.; also along Atlantic Coast from North Carolina to Georgia and Gulf Coast from n.w. Florida to Texas. **Note:** Nests inside barns and under bridges.

CLIFF SWALLOW 6"

Field Marks: Square tail; buffy rump; whitish forehead; chestnut throat; white breast and belly. **Habitat:** Farms, marshes, lakes, rivers. **Seasons:** Spring, summer, fall. **Range:** Local in distribution throughout much of East—Canada, n. U.S., and south in mountains to n. Alabama; rare and local migrant in s.e. U.S. **Note:** Nests under eaves of old unpainted barns; also on stone buildings and bridges.

PURPLE MARTIN 8"

Field Marks: Male—glossy purplish blue; female—similar but duller above; gray throat and breast; whitish belly. **Habitat:** Open country near water; farms, towns, and cities with multichambered birdhouses. **Seasons:** Spring, summer, fall. **Range:** S. Canada to Florida and Gulf of Mexico; local in much of Northeast.

Plate 22. **SWIFT, SWALLOWS**

Chimney Swift

Bank Swallow
4.

Tree Swallow
3.

Barn Swallow
1.

Cliff Swallow
2.

M.
6.

F.
5.

Purple Martin

1.   2.   3.   4.   5.   6.

Plate 23. **NIGHTJARS, HUMMINGBIRD**

COMMON NIGHTHAWK 9½"

Field Marks: Long, pointed wings; in flight, prominent white wing band. **Habitat:** Open country, over towns and cities; open pineland; wooded clearings, farms, pastures, fields. **Seasons:** Spring, summer, fall. **Range:** Canada to Florida and Gulf of Mexico.

WHIP-POOR-WILL 9½"

Field Marks: Broad rounded wings; like a huge mottled brown moth in flight. **Habitat:** Nesting—open woodland, adjacent to fields, especially oak and pine; migration—occasionally in parks, yards, and gardens. **Seasons:** Spring, summer, fall over most of area; fall, winter, spring in Deep South. **Range:** Breeds from s. Canada to coastal Virginia, mountains of n. Georgia and Alabama, and c. Arkansas; winters along Gulf of Mexico, all of Florida, and north on Atlantic Coast to Carolinas. **Note:** The Whip-poor-will is known to most people only by the familiar call of its name at night.

RUBY-THROATED HUMMINGBIRD 3½"

Field Marks: Long, slender bill; brilliant green above; male—fiery red throat; forked tail; female—all white below; square tail with white tips. **Habitat:** Gardens, orchards, woodland streams, roadside thickets with flowers—especially red, orange or yellow ones. **Seasons:** Spring, summer, fall; winter also in s. Florida. **Range:** Breeds from s. Canada to Florida and Gulf of Mexico; winters occasionally in s. Florida. **Note:** Tiny—our smallest bird. By late summer, adult males also have white throats; the feathers are molted out by that time, and both sexes appear identical, except for the tail shapes. Hummingbirds use their needle-like bills to probe into flowers. They prefer red and yellow ones—trumpet vine, hibiscus, salvia, bee balm, and jewelweed are among favorites. They are also attracted to feeders, glass tubes, or bottles containing sugar water—preferably those with red, orange, or yellow tips.

Plate 23. **NIGHTJARS, HUMMINGBIRD**

Common
Nighthawk

Common Nighthawk

Whip-poor-will

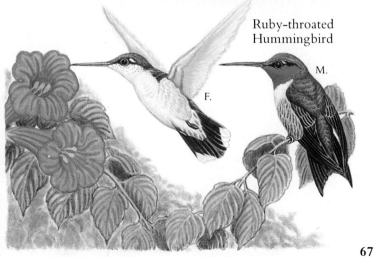

Ruby-throated
Hummingbird

F.

M.

Plate 24. **CUCKOO, PIGEONS**

YELLOW-BILLED CUCKOO 12"

Field Marks: Brown above, white below; slender, long-tailed; bill slightly downcurved, lower half yellow; large white patches on underside of tail; rufous flash in wings, evident in flight. **Habitat:** Open woodland, thickets, overgrown fields, abandoned farms, orchards. **Seasons:** Spring, summer, fall. **Range:** S. Canada to Florida and Gulf of Mexico.

MOURNING DOVE 12"

Field Marks: Slender, fawn colored; long, pointed tail, edged white. **Habitat:** Farms, suburban lawns, city parks, grasslands, roadsides. **Seasons:** All year except extreme North. **Range:** S. Canada to Florida and Gulf of Mexico. **Note:** Frequents feeders. In recent years, has become adapted to city life, even nesting on window ledges and fire escapes.

COMMON GROUND-DOVE 6½"

Field Marks: Very small; gray-brown body; short, rounded, dark tail; rufous outer wings, evident in flight; at close range, scaly head and neck. **Habitat:** Sandy fields, farms, gardens, orchards, woodland edges, beaches, roadsides. **Seasons:** All year. **Range:** Chiefly coastal lowlands from s. North Carolina to Texas; all of Florida.

ROCK (DOVE) PIGEON 13"

Field Marks: Plump, blue-gray body; short, fan-shaped tail; white rump; two black wing bars; iridescent neck patch. **Habitat:** Rock cliffs—its ancestral home; cities, towns, farms, dumps. **Seasons:** All year. **Range:** Throughout. **Note:** Introduced into North America from Europe. This is the familiar pigeon of city streets and parks, where it nests on buildings and in trees. Many color varieties occur, ranging from black to white. Also called Common Pigeon.

Plate 24. **CUCKOO, PIGEONS**

Yellow-billed Cuckoo in flight.

Yellow-billed Cuckoo

Mourning Dove

Mourning Dove in flight.

Ground-Dove in flight.

Common Ground-Dove

Rock (Dove) Pigeon in flight

Rock (Dove) Pigeon

Plate 25. **GAME BIRDS**

NORTHERN BOBWHITE 9½"

Field Marks: Small chickenlike bird; black-and-white face; female—like male, but with tawny-buff face. **Habitat:** Farmland, hedgerows, roadsides, and fields with thickets and dense brush. **Seasons:** All year. **Range:** Gulf of Mexico and Florida north to s. portions of Minnesota, Wisconsin, Michigan, and e. Great Lakes; also along East Coast lowlands to s. New England; absent from higher mountains. **Note:** Frequents feeders.

RUFFED GROUSE 17"

Field Marks: Chickenlike; black neck patch; broad black band near tail tip. **Habitat:** Open woodland; forest clearings. **Seasons:** All year. **Range:** Canada and n. U.S., west to Minnesota; south in mountains to n. Georgia and along coast to New Jersey. **Note:** Two color phases occur—gray and reddish brown.

RING-NECKED PHEASANT M. 33", F. 23"

Field Marks: Very long, pointed tail; white neck ring; iridescent purple and green head; scarlet face wattles; female—smaller and much duller; mottled brown above, tawny-buff below. **Habitat:** Farmland with hedgerows and corn fields; thickets adjacent to marshes and swamps. **Seasons:** All year. **Range:** Chiefly n. U.S. and s. Canada at low elevations, uncommon elsewhere. **Note:** Introduced from w. Asia. Frequents feeders.

WILD TURKEY M. 48", F. 36"

Field Marks: Huge, gallinaceous bird; bare head and neck with blue and red wattles; male—bristly "beard" on breast; female—smaller and somewhat duller, without much ornamentation. **Habitat:** Hardwood forest, especially foothills; wooded swamps; s.e. coastal pineland. **Seasons:** All year. **Range:** Sporadic distribution. (1) Coastal plain from Virginia to Florida, west to Mississippi; local in Louisiana and s.e. Texas. (2) Inland from s.c. New York and Pennsylvania, then chiefly west of mountains through West Virginia, Tennessee, and Alabama, west to Arkansas and Missouri. **Note:** Wild Turkeys have chestnut tail tips; domesticated varieties have white ones.

Northern
Bobwhite

Ruffed
Grouse

Plate 25. **GAMEBIRDS**

F. in flight.

Ring-necked
Pheasant

M.

Wild Turkey

Plate 26. **HAWKS 1**

BALD EAGLE 33"
> **Field Marks:** White head and tail; dark brown body and wings; large yellow bill. **Habitat:** Lakes, rivers, seacoasts; mangroves in s. Florida. **Seasons:** All year if open water is present. **Range:** Canada to Florida and Gulf of Mexico; most numerous in s. Florida; locally common in winter along Mississippi River. **Note:** Immature is *all* brown.

TURKEY VULTURE 28"
> **Field Marks:** Wings held in shallow V in flight, tilting from side to side; undersurface of wings two-toned. **Habitat:** Open country generally wherever carrion is found; in winter roosts in open woodland, especially northward. **Seasons:** All year in South; chiefly spring, summer, fall in North. **Range:** N. U.S. to Florida and Gulf of Mexico; local northward. **Note:** The bare red head of the adult somewhat resembles that of the Wild Turkey, hence its name; immature—gray head. Black Vulture also has gray head.

BLACK VULTURE 25"
> **Field Marks:** White patches near wing tips in flight seen from below; short tail; distinctive flight—several flaps and a glide; gray head at close range. **Habitat:** Farmland, fields, swamps, open pineland, woodland clearings. **Seasons:** All year. **Range:** Chiefly s.e. U.S. from Maryland, Virginia, lower Ohio and Mississippi Valleys south to Florida, Gulf of Mexico, and Texas. **Note:** Immature Turkey Vulture also has gray head.

Plate 26. **HAWKS 1**

Flight profiles.

Bald Eagle

Turkey Vulture

Black Vulture

Bald Eagle

Turkey Vulture

Black Vulture

Bald Eagle

Turkey Vulture

Black Vulture

Plate 27. **HAWKS 2**

SWALLOW-TAILED KITE 24"

Field Marks: Deeply forked tail; long, pointed wings; black and white. **Habitat:** Wooded swamps; glades; open pineland. **Seasons:** Spring, summer, fall. **Range:** All Florida; coastal plain of South Carolina, Georgia, Alabama, Mississippi and s.e. Louisiana. **Note:** Most often observed in flight.

OSPREY 24"

Field Marks: Dark above, light below; black patch at bend of wings; dark facial patch. **Habitat:** Seacoasts, lakes, rivers. **Seasons:** Spring, summer, fall; also winter in Deep South. **Range:** Breeds from Canada to Florida and Gulf of Mexico; winters in Florida, Gulf Coast, and along Atlantic Coast north to South Carolina.

NORTHERN HARRIER (MARSH HAWK) M. 19", F. 22"

Field Marks: White rump; long wings; banded tail; male—pearl gray above, pale below; female—brown above, streaked below; immature—rusty below, *no* streaks. **Habitat:** Marshes, fields, shores, beaches, sand dunes. **Seasons:** All year, but absent in winter in North in most inland areas; rare to absent in summer in South. **Range:** Canada to Florida and Gulf of Mexico.

Plate 27. **HAWKS 2**

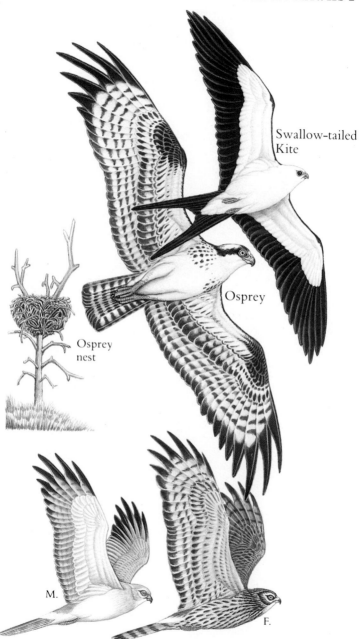

Swallow-tailed
Kite

Osprey
nest

Osprey

M.

F.

Northern Harrier (Marsh Hawk)

Plate 28. **HAWKS 3**

BROAD-WINGED HAWK 17"

Field Marks: Wide tail bands, black-and-white; white wings below; reddish body. **Habitat:** Nesting season—woodland; migration—open areas generally. **Seasons:** Spring, summer, fall; rare in winter in s. Florida. **Range:** Canada to Florida and Gulf of Mexico.

RED-SHOULDERED HAWK 21"

Field Marks: Chestnut shoulders; reddish body and wing linings; s. Florida birds much paler. **Habitat:** Low, wet woodland; wooded swamps, river bottoms. **Seasons:** All year, rare in winter northward. **Range:** S.e. Canada to Florida and Gulf of Mexico.

RED-TAILED HAWK 23"

Field Marks: Reddish tail; white breast; dark streaks on belly. **Habitat:** Woodland; groves in open country. **Seasons:** All year. **Range:** Canada to Florida and Gulf of Mexico.

ROUGH-LEGGED HAWK 23"

Field Marks: Light phase—broad, dark band near tip of white tail; dark patch at bend of mostly white wing; dark belly; dark phase—mainly black below, but with much white in wings. **Habitat:** Field, prairies, dunes, marshes, coastal areas. **Seasons:** Late fall, winter, early spring. **Range:** Canada to c. U.S., rarely farther south.

Plate 28. **HAWKS 3**

Broad-winged Hawk

Red-shouldered Hawk

Red-tailed Hawk

dark phase

light phase

Rough-legged Hawk

All hawks on this page are adults.

77

Plate 29. **HAWKS 4**

AMERICAN KESTREL (SPARROW HAWK) 11"

Field Marks: Long, pointed wings; reddish back and tail; blue-gray wings; black-and-white facial pattern; black band near tail tip; female—similar, but tail banded and wings reddish like back. **Habitat:** Farmland, fields, beaches, shores, cities. **Seasons:** All year, but rare in winter in Canada and n. U.S. **Range:** Canada to Florida and Gulf of Mexico.

MERLIN 12"

Field Marks: Long, pointed wings; heavily streaked below; banded tail; male—blue-gray above; female and immature—dark brown above. **Habitat:** Beaches, fields, marshes, thickets, light woods. **Seasons:** Summer in Canada, winter in Deep South; spring and fall throughout. **Range:** Canada to Florida and Gulf of Mexico.

SHARP-SHINNED HAWK 12"

Field Marks: Short, rounded wings; blue-gray above; rusty red below; flies with several flaps and a glide. **Habitat:** Woodland, thickets. **Seasons:** All year, but rare in winter in North and rare to absent in summer in south. **Range:** Canada to Florida and Gulf of Mexico.

Plate 29. **HAWKS 4**

M.

American Kestrel
(Sparrow Hawk)

F.

Merlin
adult

M.

imm.

Sharp-shinned Hawk
adult

Plate 30. **WOODLAND OWLS**

LONG-EARED OWL 15"

Field Marks: Head tufts close together; streaked below. **Habitat:** Forest, thickets; winter—conifer groves. **Seasons:** Chiefly fall, winter, spring in North; local in summer; winter southward. **Range:** Breeds from s. Canada to New Jersey, in mountains to Virginia; winters throughout South, but *not* Florida.

EASTERN SCREECH-OWL 9"

Field Marks: Head tufts widely spaced; streaked below; two color phases—gray and reddish brown. **Habitat:** Open woods; orchards, farm groves, shade trees; city parks, suburbs. **Seasons:** All year. **Range:** S. Canada to Florida and Gulf of Mexico.

SAW-WHET OWL 8"

Field Marks: Streaked below. **Habitat:** Summer—moist forest; winter—conifer groves in city parks and suburban yards. **Seasons:** All year in North; winter in South. **Range:** Breeds from s. Canada to New England, New York, Great Lakes region, and Illinois; mountains to West Virginia; winters south to Carolinas, Tennessee, Arkansas, rarely farther. **Note:** Our smallest owl.

GREAT HORNED OWL 22"

Field Marks: Head tufts widely spaced; white throat; barred below. **Habitat:** Forest, swampy woods; woodlots in open country; winter—large trees in city parks. **Seasons:** All year. **Range:** Canada to Florida and Gulf of Mexico.

BARRED OWL 20"

Field Marks: Dark eyes; barred throat and chest; streaked breast and belly. **Habitat:** Forest, wooded swamps, river bottoms; winter—conifer groves in parks. **Seasons:** All year. **Range:** S. Canada to Florida and Gulf of Mexico.

Plate 30.
WOODLAND OWLS

Long-eared
Owl

Eastern Screech-Owl

red phase

gray phase

Saw-whet
Owl

Great Horned
Owl

Barred
Owl

81

Plate 31. **OPEN-COUNTRY OWLS**

BURROWING OWL   10"

Field Marks: Long legs; spotted forehead; white chin; barred below.
Habitat: Ground owl; grassland; prairies, airports, bare sandy areas.
Seasons: All year in South; spring, summer, fall in Midwest. **Range:**
Florida, coastal Texas, and s.w. Louisiana; extreme w. Minnesota. **Note:**
Often seen on fence posts or on ground. When displaying or aroused,
bobs up and down.

SHORT-EARED OWL   15½"

Field Marks: Tawny-buff; heavily streaked below. **Habitat:** Fields,
prairies, marshes, dunes, beaches, airports, dumps. **Seasons:** All year in
North; fall, winter, spring southward. **Range:** Canada, n. U.S.; winters
south to Florida and Gulf of Mexico.

BARN OWL   17"

Field Marks: White heart-shaped face; pale buff below with dots; dark
eyes; long legs; slender (for an owl). **Habitat:** Chiefly open country;
large hollow trees; cliffs; old buildings; city parks. **Seasons:** All year.
Range: S. New England and New York west to s. Minnesota; south to
Florida and Gulf of Mexico. **Note:** Appears pale and ghostlike in
flight.

SNOWY OWL   23"

Field Marks: All white; sometimes heavily spotted. **Habitat:** Lake and
river shores; beaches, dunes, fields, prairies, airports, dumps, waste lots.
Seasons: Chiefly winter. **Range:** Winters south to s. Canada and n.
U.S., more rarely to c. states. **Note:** Perches on ground, poles,
haystacks, and even buildings in large cities.

Plate 31. **OPEN-COUNTRY OWLS**

Burrowing Owl

Short-eared Owl in flight.

Short-eared Owl

Barn Owl

Snowy Owl F.

Plate 32. **GEESE, SWANS**

BRANT 25"

Field Marks: Small, Mallard sized; short black neck and head; whitish below. **Habitat:** Bays, estuaries, salt marshes, tidal flats; fields, golf courses along coast. **Seasons:** Fall, winter, spring. **Range:** Mainly Atlantic Coast from w. Long Island to North Carolina; uncommon inland, but migratory flocks in Great Lakes area. **Note:** Flocks often fly low, tightly bunched in irregular formation.

CANADA GOOSE 35"

Field Marks: Long black neck and head; white chinstrap; light brown body. **Habitat:** Lakes, rivers, bays, inlets, marshes; fields, golf courses, large lawns. **Seasons:** Fall, winter, spring; few in summer. **Range:** Canada to Florida and Gulf of Mexico. **Note:** Largest goose. During migration flocks fly high in long V-shaped formation, honking noisily.

SNOW GOOSE 30"

Field Marks: Medium sized; white with much black in wings; imma-ture—pale gray. **Habitat:** Marshes, ponds, bays; cutover grain fields, golf courses. **Seasons:** Fall, winter, spring. **Range:** Canada to Gulf of Mexico; rare on Atlantic Coast south of North Carolina. **Note:** The so-called Blue Goose is the dark phase; dark grayish brown with white head and upper neck. Numerous on Great Lakes, Mississippi River, Gulf Coast of Louisiana and Texas; uncommon near Atlantic Coast.

TUNDRA (WHISTLING) SWAN 53"

Field Marks: All white; long, straight neck; black bill; immature—dull brown; pinkish bill. **Habitat:** Lakes, rivers, bays, flooded fields. **Seasons:** Fall, winter, spring. **Range:** Atlantic Coast from Maryland to North Carolina; migratory flocks in Great Lakes area. **Note:** Smaller than Mute Swan

MUTE SWAN 60"

Field Marks: All white; graceful curved neck; orange bill pointing down; black knob at base of bill; immature—dull brown; pinkish bill, black at base, no knob. **Habitat:** Ponds, marshes, bays. **Seasons:** All year. **Range:** East Coast from Massachusetts to Maryland; uncommon elsewhere. **Note:** Our largest waterfowl. The familiar swan of parks and estates. Introduced from Europe.

Plate 32. **GEESE, SWANS**

Brant
in flight.

Canada
Goose

Canada Geese
in flight.

Brant

Snow Goose

imm.
white
phase

adult
blue phase

adult
white phase

Tundra
(Whistling)
Swan

adult

imm.

adult in flight

imm.

Mute
Swan

adult

Plate 33. **TIPPING DUCKS 1**

NORTHERN PINTAIL 27"

Field Marks: White vertical line on side of head; white neck and breast; dark brown head and hindneck; gray body; long, pointed tail; female—mottled brown. **Habitat:** Marshes, ponds, rivers. **Seasons:** Fall, winter, spring; local in summer in North. **Range:** Canada to Florida and Gulf of Mexico.

GADWALL 21"

Field Marks: Dark gray, with brown head and neck; chestnut and white wing patch evident in flight; female—brown with wing patch. **Habitat:** Marshes, ponds, rivers. **Seasons:** Fall, winter, spring; local in summer in North. **Range:** Canada to Florida and Gulf of Mexico.

AMERICAN BLACK DUCK 24"

Field Marks: Dark brown (black at a distance); head and neck light brown; greenish yellow bill; violet wing patch evident in flight. **Habitat:** Marshes, ponds, lakes, rivers, bays, estuaries. **Seasons:** All year in North; fall, winter, spring in South. **Range:** Canada to c. Florida and Gulf of Mexico. **Note:** Generally replaces Mallard in winter along North Atlantic coast.

MALLARD 24"

Field Marks: Bright green head; yellow bill; white neck ring; chestnut breast; blue wing patch bordered with white bars; female—mottled brown; orange bill with brown patch. **Habitat:** Marshes, ponds, lakes, rivers, bays, flooded fields. **Seasons:** All year. **Range:** Canada to Florida and Gulf of Mexico. **Note:** The common all-white Pekin Duck or so-called Long Island Duck (see illustration) is a domesticated derivative of the wild Mallard. It is often larger, with bright orange bill and feet; frequents barnyard ponds and waterfowl preserves and associates with Mallards.

MUSCOVY DUCK 29"

Field Marks: White, black, or combination of both; large white wing patch; red warty knob at base of bill and bare skin around eye. **Habitat:** Ornamental waterfowl ponds; barnyard pools. **Seasons:** All year. **Range:** Introduced from tropical America into U.S., where it has become established and semidomesticated. **Note:** This stocky, ungainly looking waterfowl is often found with Mallards but is larger and gooselike in appearance.

Plate 33. **TIPPING DUCKS 1**

Pintail

M.

F.

Gadwall

M.

F.

Black
Duck

Mallard

F.

M.

Pekin Duck

Muscovy Duck

Mallard

Use the Mallard (in smaller
scale below) for size comparison of Pekin and Muscovy
Ducks with larger figures
above.

87

Plate 34. **TIPPING DUCKS 2**

NORTHERN SHOVELER 20"

Field Marks: Long shovel-shaped bill pointed down; green head; chestnut sides; white chest; light blue wing patch evident in flight; female—light brown with wing patch. **Habitat:** Marshes, ponds; winter—estuaries, shallow bays. **Seasons:** Fall, winter, spring; local in summer in North. **Range:** Breeds locally in Minnesota, Wisconsin, and Iowa, rare farther east; winters mainly along Atlantic Coast from Long Island to Florida, along Gulf Coast, and Mississippi Valley north to Ohio River.

BLUE-WINGED TEAL 16"

Field Marks: White crescent behind bill; light blue wing patch evident in flight; female—all brown, with wing patch. **Habitat:** Marshes, ponds, lagoons. **Seasons:** Spring, summer, fall; winters in South. **Range:** S. Canada to Florida and Gulf of Mexico.

GREEN-WINGED TEAL 14"

Field Marks: Chestnut head with green patch; white vertical line in front of wing; gray body; green wing patch evident in flight; female—light brown with wing patch. **Habitat:** Marshes, ponds, estuaries. **Seasons:** Fall, winter, spring; summer in n. U.S. and s. Canada. **Range:** Canada to Florida and Gulf of Mexico. **Note:** On the water the females of the two teals are impossible to tell apart.

AMERICAN WIGEON (BALDPATE) 20"

Field Marks: White forecrown; green head patch; white wing patch evident in flight; female—brownish with gray head; wing patch. **Habitat:** Marshes, ponds, lakes, rivers, lagoons, bays, estuaries. **Seasons:** Fall, winter, spring; uncommon in summer. **Range:** Winters along Gulf Coast; north in Mississippi Valley to Ohio River; along Atlantic Coast from Florida to Long Island, uncommonly to s. New England; local in summer in n. U.S. and s. Canada. **Note:** Although officially called American Wigeon, "Baldpate" is much more apt in reference to its white forecrown.

WOOD DUCK 18½"

Field Marks: Gaudily colored in green, purple, blue, and white; chestnut breast; red eye and base of bill; swept-back crest; female—dull, mostly grayish; prominent white eye patch. **Habitat:** Swamps, marshes, ponds, streams. **Seasons:** All year, but rare and local in winter in North. **Range:** S. Canada to Florida and Gulf of Mexico; winters mainly in South. **Note:** Hole nester in tree cavities and nest boxes.

Plate 34. **TIPPING DUCKS 2**

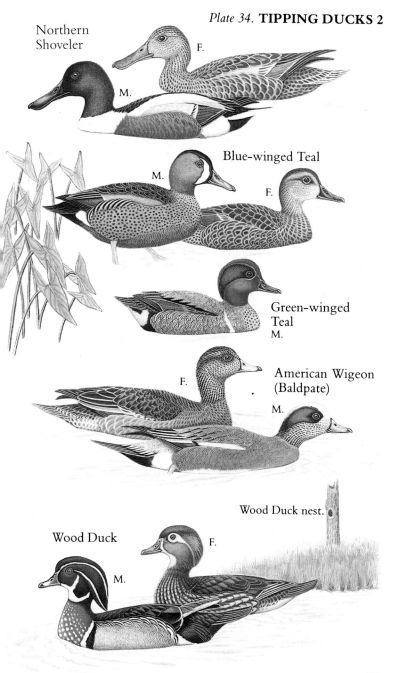

Northern
Shoveler

F.

M.

Blue-winged Teal

M.

F.

Green-winged
Teal
M.

American Wigeon
(Baldpate)

F.

M.

Wood Duck nest.

Wood Duck

F.

M.

Plate 35. **DIVING DUCKS 1**

CANVASBACK 22"

Field Marks: White body; chestnut head and neck; black chest; sloping profile; long bill; female—much duller grayish brown. **Habitat:** Lakes, rivers, marshes, bays, estuaries. **Seasons:** Fall, winter, spring. **Range:** Canada to Florida and Gulf of Mexico.

REDHEAD 20"

Field Marks: Gray body; reddish head and neck; black chest; rounded profile; short bill; female—dull brownish. **Habitat:** Lakes, rivers, marshes, bays, estuaries. **Seasons:** Fall, winter, spring. **Range:** Canada to Florida and Gulf of Mexico.

RING-NECKED DUCK 16½"

Field Marks: Black head, back and breast; white wedge in front of wing; pale blue bill with white ring and black tip; pale gray sides; close up—purplish gloss on head; female—brownish with white eye ring. **Habitat:** Wooded ponds, lakes, reservoirs, rivers; winter in South—also salt lagoons, coastal estuaries. **Seasons:** Fall, winter, spring, local in summer in extreme North. **Range:** Canada to Florida and Gulf of Mexico.

GREATER AND LESSER SCAUP 18" and 16½"

Field Marks: Black fore and aft; light in the middle; close up—profile only, head of Greater, green; head of Lesser, purple; females—brownish, with distinct white patch at base of bill; indistinguishable from each other on water. **Habitat:** Lakes, rivers, bays, estuaries; Greater Scaup also in ocean and Gulf of Mexico. **Seasons:** Fall, winter, spring. **Range:** Canada to Florida and Gulf of Mexico; during winter, Greaters occur chiefly in salt water in Northeast; Lessers occur both inland in s. states and on saltwater bays in Florida and along Gulf of Mexico.

RUDDY DUCK 15½"

Field Marks: Male, spring/summer—white cheek; bright blue bill; chestnut body; dark cap; cocks tail up into a fan; fall/winter—dull brown body, gray bill; female—similar to winter male but cheek has dark horizontal stripe. **Habitat:** Marshes, ponds, lakes, lagoons, bays, estuaries. **Seasons:** Fall, winter, spring; very local in summer. **Range:** Local breeder in Northeast; migrates and winters chiefly along Atlantic Coast from New York to Florida, west through Gulf states and lower Mississippi Valley.

Plate 35. **DIVIN**

Canvasba

F.

M.

F. Redhead

M.

Ring-necked Duck

M. F.

Greater Scaup

M.

Lesser Scaup

M.

F.

Ruddy Duck

M. F.

COMMON GOLDENEYE 20"

Field Marks: Dark, puffy head; white body; white patch behind bill; black back; close up—green gloss on head; bright yellow eye; female—gray body and dark head separated by white collar. **Habitat:** Lakes, rivers, bays, inlets, estuaries. **Seasons:** Fall, winter, spring. **Range:** Canada to Florida and Gulf of Mexico.

BUFFLEHEAD 14"

Field Marks: Large white patch on dark head; white body; black back; close up—iridescent green and purple head; female—small white patch on dark head behind eye; grayish body. **Habitat:** Lakes, rivers, bays, inlets, estuaries. **Seasons:** Fall, winter, spring. **Range:** Canada to Florida and Gulf of Mexico.

HOODED MERGANSER 17½"

Field Marks: Fan-shaped white crest with black border; rusty sides; white breast with two vertical black stripes; black face, neck, back; female—smaller, dull grayish brown; swept-back reddish brown crest. **Habitat:** Wooded lakes, ponds, streams; in winter, especially in the South—also salt creeks, bays, estuaries. **Seasons:** Fall, winter, spring; local in summer. **Range:** Canada to Florida and Gulf of Mexico.

RED-BREASTED MERGANSER 22"

Field Marks: Swept-back crest; red bill; white collar; rusty chest; black back; close up—glossy dark green head; female—reddish neck and crested head, the former blending with white throat and breast. **Habitat:** Winter—chiefly coastal waters, including ocean; migration and summer—large lakes and rivers. **Seasons:** Fall, winter, spring; in summer, local in North. **Range:** Canada to Florida and Gulf of Mexico.

COMMON MERGANSER 25"

Field Marks: Dark, glossy green head; white body; red bill; black back; female—similar to female Red-breasted Merganser, but reddish neck contrasts sharply with white chest. **Habitat:** Lakes, reservoirs, rivers, bays in winter. **Seasons:** Fall, winter, spring; in summer, local in North. **Range:** Canada to Gulf states, but rare south of Carolinas and n. Louisiana.

Plate 36. **DIVING DUCKS 2**

Common Goldeneye

F.

M.

Bufflehead

F.

M.

Hooded
Merganser

M.

F.

Red-breasted
Merganser

M.

F.

Common
Merganser

M.

F.

Plate 37. **DIVING DUCKS 3**

WHITE-WINGED SCOTER 21"

Field Marks: Black sea duck; small white face patch; orange bill with black knob at base; white wing patch evident in flight; female—sooty brown with white wing patch; two circular dull white head patches; dark bill. **Habitat:** Ocean, bays, large lakes, rivers. **Seasons:** Fall, winter, spring. **Range:** Winters chiefly on Atlantic Coast from Canada to North Carolina; in migration also on Great Lakes.

SURF SCOTER 19"

Field Marks: Black sea duck; two white head patches; bill black, white and reddish; female—identical to female White-winged Scoter, but no wing patch. **Habitat:** Ocean, bays, large lakes, rivers. **Seasons:** Fall, winter, spring. **Range:** Winters mainly on Atlantic Coast from Canada to Florida; in migration also on Great Lakes.

BLACK SCOTER 18"

Field Marks: All-black sea duck; large orange knob on black bill; female—like other female scoters, but entire face and throat whitish. **Habitat:** Ocean, bays, large lakes, rivers. **Seasons:** Fall, winter, spring. **Range:** Winters chiefly on Atlantic Coast from Canada to South Carolina; in migration also on Great Lakes.

OLDSQUAW M. 20", F. 16"

Field Marks: Boldly patterned in dark brown and white; dark cheek patch; long, pointed tail; pinkish bill with dark tip and base; female—white face and neck with small, dark cheek spot; short pointed tail. **Habitat:** Ocean, inlets, bays, large lakes, rivers. **Seasons:** Fall, winter, spring. **Range:** Winters chiefly on Atlantic Coast from Canada to Virginia; in migration and winter also on Great Lakes.

COMMON EIDER 25"

Field Marks: Large black-and-white sea duck; head with long, sloping profile; thick neck; female—dull brown with dark barring; immature—dark brown body with white breast. **Habitat:** Ocean, rocky coasts, shoals. **Seasons:** Fall, winter, spring; local in summer. **Range:** Breeds on Atlantic Coast from Canada to c. Maine; winters south to e. Long Island.

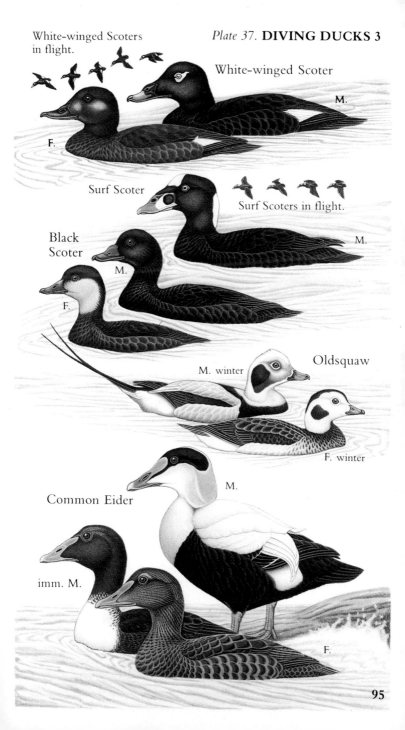

White-winged Scoters in flight.

Plate 37. **DIVING DUCKS 3**

White-winged Scoter

M.

F.

Surf Scoter

Surf Scoters in flight.

M.

Black Scoter

M.

F.

Oldsquaw

M. winter

F. winter

Common Eider

M.

imm. M.

F.

Plate 38. **RAILS, COOT, GALLINULES**

CLAPPER RAIL 15"

Field Marks: Chickenlike; long, slender, slightly curved bill; grayish brown; gray cheeks; barred gray and white sides. **Habitat:** Salt marshes, mangroves in s. Florida. **Seasons:** All year in South; chiefly spring, summer, fall in North. **Range:** Atlantic and Gulf coasts from Long Island to Florida and Texas; local north to Cape Cod. **Note:** Often can be located by distinctive call—"cack, cack, cack."

VIRGINIA RAIL 9"

Field Marks: Chickenlike; long, slender, slightly curved bill; reddish with gray cheeks; barred black-and-white sides. **Habitat:** Fresh and brackish marshes; winter—chiefly coastal salt marshes. **Seasons:** Spring, summer, fall in North; fall, winter, spring in South. **Range:** S. Canada to Florida and Gulf of Mexico; breeds primarily in North; winters mainly in South; rarely along Atlantic Coast to New England.

AMERICAN COOT 14½"

Field Marks: Deep gray with white bill. **Habitat:** Marshes, ponds, lakes, lawns, fields, bays. **Seasons:** All year, but local in winter inland; north along coast to Massachusetts. **Range:** S. Canada to Florida and Gulf of Mexico. **Note:** Swims with head bobbing back and forth.

PURPLE GALLINULE 13"

Field Marks: Vivid purple head and underparts; red bill with yellow tip; light blue forehead; bronze-green back; bright yellow legs. **Habitat:** Marshes, swamps, ponds. **Seasons:** All year (see winter range below). **Range:** Coastal South Carolina to Florida, west to Texas; Mississippi Valley from Gulf of Mexico to Arkansas and s.w. Tennessee; winters in Florida and along coasts of Louisiana and Texas. **Note:** Often climbs bushes.

COMMON MOORHEN (COMMON GALLINULE) 13"

Field Marks: Red forehead and bill with yellow tip; deep gray head and body; brown back; narrow white side stripe. **Habitat:** Marshes, ponds, lawns near water. **Range:** From s. Canada and n. U.S. to Florida and Gulf of Mexico. **Note:** Swims with head bobbing back and forth.

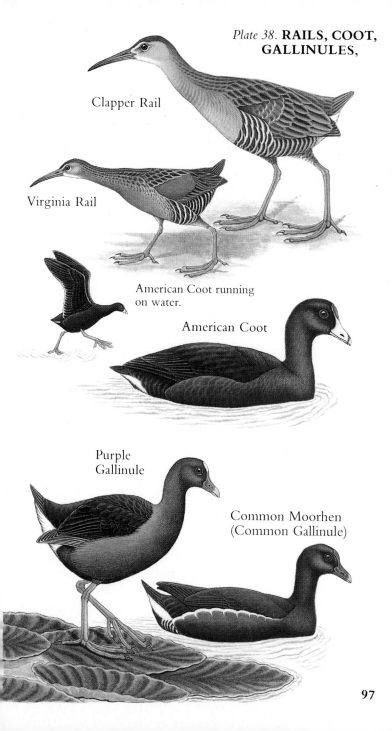

Plate 38. **RAILS, COOT, GALLINULES,**

Clapper Rail

Virginia Rail

American Coot running on water.

American Coot

Purple Gallinule

Common Moorhen (Common Gallinule)

Plate 39. **GREBES**

PIED-BILLED GREBE 13"

Field Marks: Spring/summer—black ring on thick whitish bill; brownish body with black throat; fall/winter—similar, but *no* black. **Habitat:** Marshes, weedy ponds, lakes; bays in winter. **Seasons:** All year, but rare and local in winter in North. **Range:** S. Canada to Florida and Gulf of Mexico.

HORNED GREBE 13½"

Field Marks: Spring/summer—golden ear tufts; black head and back; chestnut neck; fall/winter—black above, white below. **Habitat:** Lakes, ponds, rivers, bays, inlets, ocean. **Seasons:** Fall, winter, spring. **Range:** Canada to Florida and Gulf of Mexico; breeds locally within our area in w. Ontario and n.w. Minnesota.

RED-NECKED GREBE 18"

Field Marks: Yellowish dark-tipped bill; spring/summer—black cap; whitish cheek and throat; reddish neck; fall/winter—grayish; white crescent on grayish cheek. **Habitat:** Lakes, ponds, rivers, bays, inlets, ocean. **Seasons:** Chiefly fall, winter, spring; summer in Ontario and Minnesota. **Range:** Breeds in w. Ontario and Minnesota; migrates via Great Lakes and upper Minnesota Valley east toward Atlantic Coast; winters on coast from Nova Scotia to e. Long Island, rarely south to Georgia.

Plate 39. **GREBES**

summer

Pied-billed Grebe

winter

Horned Grebe

winter

summer

summer

Red-necked Grebe

winter

Plate 40. **GUILLEMOT, LOONS**

BLACK GUILLEMOT 13"

Field Marks: Small, chunky, duck like seabird; large white wing patch; pointed bill; spring/summer—black; fall/winter—white head, neck and below. **Habitat:** Rocky seacoasts and islands; inshore ocean waters. **Seasons:** All year. **Range:** Coastal; Canada and Maine, rarely south to Massachusetts.

RED-THROATED LOON 25"

Field Marks: Sharp, pointed bill tilted upward; summer—gray head; reddish throat; dark above, white below; fall/winter/spring—head and neck pale. **Habitat:** Lakes, reservoirs, rivers, estuaries, bays, inlets, ocean. **Seasons:** Chiefly fall, winter, spring. **Range:** Canada to Florida and Gulf of Mexico, both inland and coastal. **Note:** Rarely seen during breeding season in our area.

COMMON LOON 32"

Field Marks: Spring/summer—back and sides blotched black and white; black head and neck; white below; long, sharply pointed bill; fall/winter—dark above, white below. **Habitat:** Summer—wooded lakes; fall/winter/spring—rivers, lakes, reservoirs, bays, ocean. **Seasons:** Spring, summer, fall northward; late fall, winter, early spring southward; also winters north on ocean. **Range:** Summer—Canada, n. U.S.; winter—south to Florida and Gulf of Mexico.

Plate 40. **GUILLEMOT, LOONS**

summer

Black Guillemot

winter

summer

Red-throated Loon

winter

winter

Common Loon

summer

Plate 41. **CORMORANTS, ANHINGA**

GREAT CORMORANT 37"

Field Marks: All-black plumage; white cheeks and chin; yellow pouch; breeding adult has white flank evident in flight; immature— sooty brown with white belly. **Habitat:** Rocky coast and islands. **Seasons:** All year in Canada; chiefly in winter from Maine to New Jersey. **Range:** Coastal; breeds in s. Canada; winters south to New Jersey.

DOUBLE-CRESTED CORMORANT 33"

Field Marks: All-black plumage; orange chin pouch; immature— sooty brown with whitish throat and breast. **Habitat:** Coastal bays and islands; inland lakes and rivers. **Seasons:** Spring, summer, fall in North; winter in South, but all year in Florida and on coast north to Carolinas. **Range:** S. Canada to Florida and Gulf of Mexico.

NEOTROPIC (OLIVACEOUS) CORMORANT 25"

Field Marks: All-black plumage; yellowish pouch; white chin in breeding season. **Habitat:** Tidal lagoons, lakes, coastal thickets. **Seasons:** All year. **Range:** Coasts of Texas and s.w. Louisiana.

ANHINGA 34"

Field Marks: Male—black with silvery white wing patches; female— black body with light brown head, neck, and chest. **Habitat:** Wooded ponds, swamps, rivers, cypress backwaters, rice fields. **Seasons:** All year in Florida and along both coasts; spring, summer, fall in North Carolina and other inland areas. **Range:** S. Atlantic and Gulf states, from North Carolina to Texas, mainly near coast, but throughout Florida and Louisiana; north in Mississippi Valley to Arkansas and Tennessee.

imm.
Great Cormorant

Plate 41.
**CORMORANTS,
ANHINGA**

Great
Cormorant
adult

imm.
Double-crested
Cormorant

Double-crested
Cormorant
adult

Neotropic (Olivaceous)
Cormorant

adult F.
in flight

adult male   Anhinga

imm.

Plate 42. **GANNET, PELICANS, FRIGATEBIRD**

NORTHERN GANNET 38"

Field Marks: Large white seabird, much larger than any gull; black wing tips; wedge-shaped tail; immature—all dark with white speckles or, in older birds, black-and-white blotches. **Habitat:** Sea cliffs, ocean. **Seasons:** Fall, winter, spring; summer on breeding grounds. **Range:** Breeds in large colonies on sea cliffs, as on Bonaventure Island, Quebec; during migration and in winter from Cape Cod to Florida, more rarely Gulf of Mexico.

WHITE PELICAN 62"

Field Marks: Huge white bird; very long orange bill; much black in wings, evident in flight. **Habitat:** Lakes, marshes, shallow bays, shores, beaches. **Seasons:** Fall, winter, spring in South; summer in Northwest. **Range:** Winters chiefly along coast from s. Florida to Texas; migrates mainly through Mississippi Valley from main breeding grounds in w. Canada and extreme w. Minnesota.

MAGNIFICENT FRIGATEBIRD 40"

Field Marks: Large black seabird with extremely long wings and deeply forked tail; long, hooked bill; adult male—all-black plumage with scarlet throat pouch, inflated when displaying; adult female—black with white breast; immature—similar but entire head, neck and breast white. **Habitat:** Ocean, open gulf, mangroves, bays, islands. **Seasons:** All year. **Range:** S. Atlantic and Gulf coasts of Florida; most numerous in Florida Keys, north to Miami; less frequent in Gulf of Mexico west to Texas.

BROWN PELICAN 50"

Field Marks: Very large grayish brownish bird; very long grayish white bill; white head; immature—all brown. **Habitat:** Ocean, bays, inlets, beaches, mangroves. **Seasons:** All year in Florida; chiefly spring, summer, fall elsewhere. **Range:** Coastal; chiefly Florida, ranging north to Carolinas, but local along Gulf west of Florida as far as Texas.

Plate 42. **GANNET, PELICANS, FRIGATEBIRD**

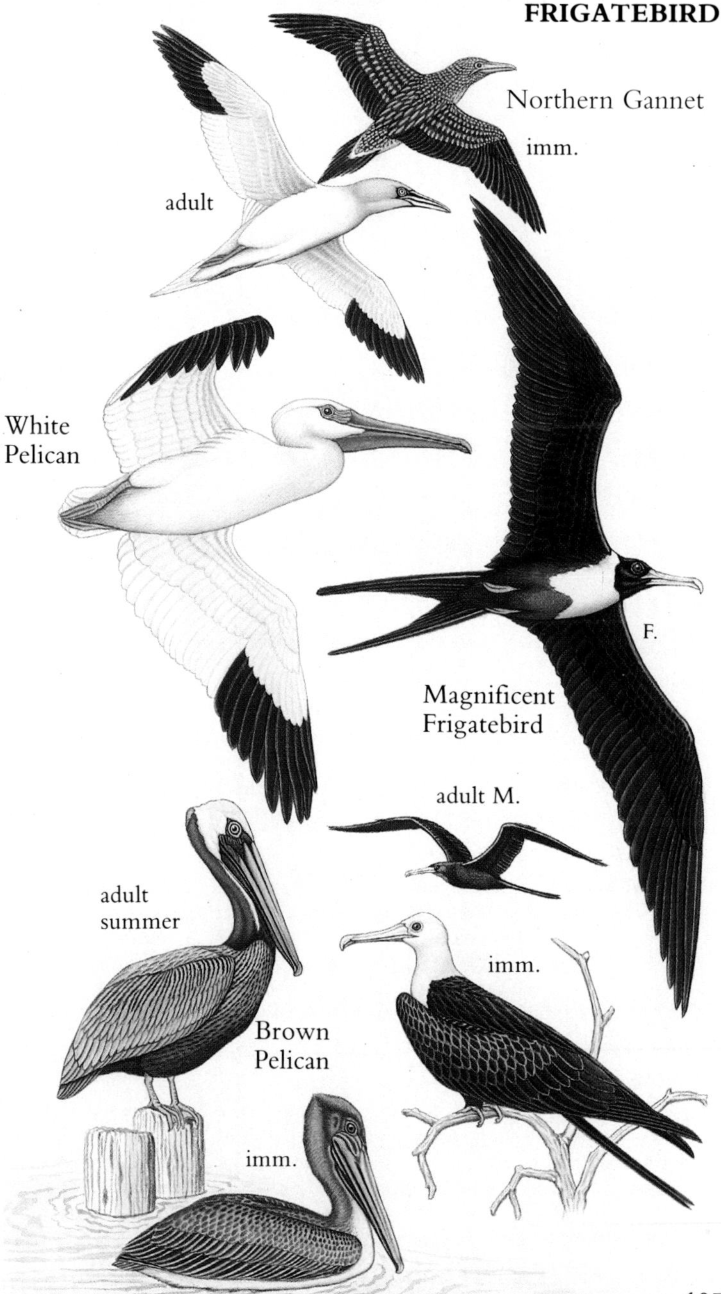

Northern Gannet

imm.

adult

White
Pelican

Magnificent
Frigatebird

F.

adult M.

imm.

Brown
Pelican

adult
summer

imm.

105

Plate 43. **WHITE HERONS**

"GREAT WHITE" HERON 50"

Field Marks: All white plumage; yellow bill; yellowish legs. **Habitat:** Shallow bays, mangroves, tidal flats. **Seasons:** All year. **Range:** Florida Bay and Keys. **Note:** Considered to be the white form of the Great Blue Heron; intermediate color forms also occur within this range.

GREAT EGRET 38"

Field Marks: All white plumage; yellow bill; black legs. **Habitat:** Marshes, swamps, ponds, bays, tidal flats. **Seasons:** All year in South; spring, summer, fall elsewhere. **Range:** Along coast from Long Island to Florida and Texas; inland from Gulf states to s. Minnesota, Wisconsin, and Ohio; local farther north; winters along Atlantic and Gulf Coasts from Carolinas to Texas.

REDDISH EGRET (White phase) 29"

Field Marks: All white plumage; pinkish bill, tipped black; bluish legs. **Habitat:** Florida—shallow bays, mangroves; Texas—lagoons, coastal scrub. **Seasons:** All year, but scarcer in winter. **Range:** Florida Bay and Keys; Texas coast; uncommon along Gulf coast of Louisiana, east to n.w. Florida. **Note:** This bird occurs in two color forms. For dark phase, see Plate 44.

CATTLE EGRET 20"

Field Marks: Stocky, thick neck; spring/summer—golden buff plumes on head, breast, and back; short orange-red bill, reddish legs; fall/winter—all white plumage; yellow bill, greenish legs. **Habitat:** Fields, farms, airports, golf courses, lawns. **Seasons:** All year in South; spring, summer, fall elsewhere. **Range:** Chiefly along coast from s. New Jersey to Florida and Texas; local elsewhere, but increasing; winters in Florida and along Gulf Coast, especially Louisiana and Texas. **Note:** Often associates with cattle and other livestock.

LITTLE BLUE HERON (Immature) 24"

Field Marks: All white plumage; bluish gray bill tipped black; greenish legs. **Habitat:** Marshes, swamps, ponds, rice fields, lagoons, tidal flats, shallow bays. **Seasons:** All year in South; spring, summer, fall elsewhere. **Range:** Chiefly coastal, from Long Island to Florida and Texas; also inland in Gulf states and Mississippi Valley north to Missouri and Illinois; local farther north; winters on coast from Carolinas to Florida and Texas. **Note:** For dark adult, see Plate 44.

SNOWY EGRET 23"

Field Marks: All white plumage; black bill and legs; yellow feet. **Habitat:** Marshes, swamps, ponds, rice fields, shallow bays, tidal flats. **Seasons:** All year in South; spring, summer, fall elsewhere. **Range:** Along coast from Long Island to Florida and Texas; inland along Mississippi River from Gulf of Mexico to Arkansas and Tennessee; local farther north; winters north to Maryland.

Plate 43.
WHITE HERONS

"Great White" Heron

Great Egret

Reddish Egret

white phase

Cattle Egret

imm.

adult

Little Blue Heron imm.

Snowy Egret

Plate 44. **CRANE, DARK HERONS 1**

SANDHILL CRANE 45"

Field Marks: Very large; all gray plumage; bare red crown; black legs. **Habitat:** Prairies, fields, swales, marshes. **Seasons:** All year in Florida; spring, summer, fall elsewhere. **Range:** Local; breeds in Canada, Minnesota, Wisconsin, Michigan, s.e. Florida; migrates via w. Great Lakes and Mississippi Valley. **Note:** Flies with neck outstretched.

GREAT BLUE HERON 44"

Field Marks: Very large; bluish gray; whitish head; black head plumes. **Habitat:** Marshes, swamps, lakes, rivers, tidal flats. **Seasons:** All year, but scarcer in winter in North. **Range:** S. Canada to Florida and Gulf of Mexico. **Note:** Flies with neck folded in.

LITTLE BLUE HERON (Adult) 24"

Field Marks: Slate blue body; maroon head and neck; bluish gray bill tipped black; greenish legs. **Habitat:** Marshes, swamps, ponds, rice, fields, lagoons, shallow bays, tidal flats. **Seasons:** All year in South; spring, summer, fall elsewhere. **Range:** Breeds along coast from Long Island to Florida and Texas; also inland from Florida to Texas and up Mississippi Valley to Missouri and Illinois; local farther north; winters on coast from Carolinas to Florida and Texas. **Note:** For white immature, see Plate 43.

REDDISH EGRET (Dark phase) 29"

Field Marks: Slate gray body; rufous head and neck; pinkish bill, tipped black; bluish legs. **Habitat:** Florida—shallow bays, mangroves; Texas—lagoons, coastal scrub. **Seasons:** All year, but scarcer in winter. **Range:** Florida Bay and Keys; Texas coast; uncommon along Gulf coast of Louisiana, east to n.w. Florida. **Note:** This species occurs in two color forms. For white phase, see Plate 43.

TRICOLORED (LOUISIANA) HERON 26"

Field Marks: Purplish blue with white belly; bright blue bill in breeding season, duller at other times; very slender heron with snake like neck. **Habitat:** Marshes, swamps, bayous, mangroves, lagoons, tidal flats. **Seasons:** All year in South; spring, summer, fall in North as far as Long Island. **Range:** Coast, chiefly from s. New Jersey to Florida (entire state) and Texas; local farther north.

Plate 44. **CRANE, DARK HERONS 1**

Sandhill Crane

Great
Blue Heron

Sandhill Crane
in flight.

Great Blue
Heron
in flight.

Little
Blue Heron
adult

Tricolored
(Louisiana)
Heron

Reddish Egret
dark phase

Plate 45. **DARK HERONS 2**

YELLOW-CROWNED NIGHT-HERON 25"

Field Marks: Stocky; black-and-white head; gray body; two short, yellowish white head plumes in breeding season. **Habitat:** In South— mangroves, cypress swamps, bayous; elsewhere—salt marshes, wooded ponds, streams, coastal thickets. **Seasons:** Spring, summer, fall; all year in Florida and Gulf Coast. **Range:** Chiefly s. U.S., ranging north along coast to Long Island and up Mississippi Valley to s. portions of Minnesota and Wisconsin; winters chiefly in Florida and along Gulf Coast to Texas. **Note:** Immatures of both Night Herons virtually alike.

BLACK-CROWNED NIGHT-HERON 25"

Field Marks: Stocky; black cap and back; two long white head plumes in breeding season; gray wings; white below; immature—brown, streaked, and spotted. **Habitat:** Marshes, swamps, wooded ponds, streams, tidal flats. **Seasons:** All year, but local in winter in North. **Range:** S. Canada to Florida and Gulf of Mexico; most numerous along coast, local inland in North.

AMERICAN BITTERN 23"

Field Marks: Stocky; tawny-brown with dark streaks below, blending with reeds; black neck stripe; blackish outer wings evident in flight. **Habitat:** Marshes, wet meadows, bogs. **Seasons:** Warmer months in North, colder months in South. **Range:** Canada to Florida and Gulf of Mexico; winters mainly in South.

LEAST BITTERN 13"

Field Marks: Greenish black above; buff wing patch; tawny sides of head and neck. **Habitat:** Freshwater and brackish marshes, especially where cattails are present. **Seasons:** Spring, summer, fall; all year in s. Florida and coastal Texas. **Range:** S. Canada to Florida and Gulf of Mexico; winters in s. Florida, locally in large numbers. **Note:** Our smallest heron.

GREEN HERON 18"

Field Marks: Chestnut head and neck; back and wings bluish gray, back with green sheen; greenish yellow legs; immature duller with streaked neck. **Habitat:** Marshes, swamps, wooded ponds, streams, coastal thickets. **Seasons:** Spring, summer, fall; all year in Florida and along Gulf and s. Atlantic Coasts. **Range:** S. Canada to Florida and Gulf of Mexico; winters mainly in Florida and along Gulf Coast to Texas, uncommon north to South Carolina.

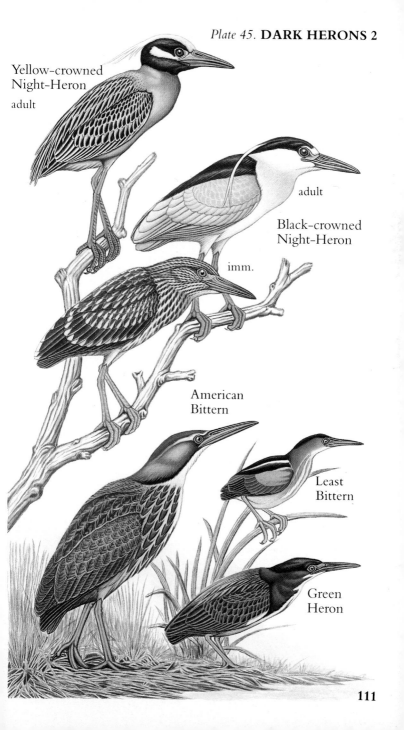

Plate 45. **DARK HERONS 2**

Yellow-crowned
Night-Heron

adult

adult

Black-crowned
Night-Heron

imm.

American
Bittern

Least
Bittern

Green
Heron

Plate 46. # STORK, IBISES, SPOONBILL, LIMPKIN

WOOD STORK 42"

Field Marks: Large white bird; bare head and dark gray neck; heavy dark bill, slightly decurved; black legs; much black in wings evident in flight; immature—yellow bill. **Habitat:** Cypress swamps, wooded ponds, marshes, lagoons, mangroves. **Seasons:** All year, but wanders widely after nesting season. **Range:** Over much of Florida except extreme north; s.e. Georgia; local throughout.

WHITE IBIS 25"

Field Marks: White bird; bright red face, decurved bill and legs; black wing tips in flight. Immature—brown above, white below. **Habitat:** Marshes, rice fields, lagoons, mangroves. **Seasons:** All year. **Range:** All Florida; Atlantic Coast to North Carolina; Virginia in recent years; Gulf Coast to Texas.

GLOSSY IBIS 24"

Field Marks: Black at distance; slender decurved bill; in good light or close up—iridescent bronze-green, chestnut, and purple. **Habitat:** Marshes, swamps, rice fields, coastal flats, estuaries. **Seasons:** All year in s. Atlantic and Gulf states; spring, summer, fall farther north. **Range:** Coast from Texas to Florida (inland in Florida also), north to Long Island, rarely to Maine; winters from Carolinas southward.

LIMPKIN 28"

Field Marks: Dark brown; white spots and streaks; slender bill, slightly decurved. **Habitat:** Wooded swamps, marshes. **Seasons:** All year. **Range:** Through much of Florida but local, absent from panhandle and n.e. portion; uncommon in s.e. Georgia.

ROSEATE SPOONBILL 32"

Field Marks: Brilliant pink and white; flattened yellow-green bill with spoon-shaped tip; immature—white with pale bill. **Habitat:** Mangroves, coastal swamps, salt marshes, mud flats. **Seasons:** All year. **Range:** Southern third of Florida; Texas coast.

Plate 46. **STORK, IBISES, SPOONBILL, LIMPKIN**

Wood Stork in flight.

adult White Ibis in flight.

Wood Stork

White Ibis imm.

Glossy Ibis

Limpkin

adult

Roseate Spoonbill

imm.

Plate 47. **SHOREBIRDS 1**

AMERICAN AVOCET 18"

Field Marks: Flashy black-and-white wings; long, slender, upturned black bill; blue-gray legs; spring/summer—rusty head and neck, fall/winter—pale gray. **Habitat:** Shallow lakes, open marshes, shores, flats. **Seasons:** All year in Texas; spring, summer, fall elsewhere. **Range:** Resident on Texas coast; local migrant and winter visitant on Gulf Coast from Florida to Louisiana; sporadic on Atlantic Coast north to s. New Jersey.

BLACK-NECKED STILT 15"

Field Marks: Black above, white below; long red legs; thin black bill. **Habitat:** Open marshes, shallow lakes and pools, tidal flats, estuaries. **Seasons:** All year in extreme South; spring, summer, fall elsewhere. **Range:** Local breeder on Atlantic and Gulf Coasts from Delaware to Florida and Texas; inland also in c. and s. Florida.

AMERICAN OYSTERCATCHER 19"

Field Marks: Dark above, white below; heavy red bill; flesh-colored legs. **Habitat:** Tidal mud flats, sand and shell beaches. **Seasons:** All year in South; spring, summer, fall northward. **Range:** Gulf and Atlantic Coasts from Texas to Florida and Virginia; local north to Long Island.

Plate 47. **SHOREBIRDS 1**

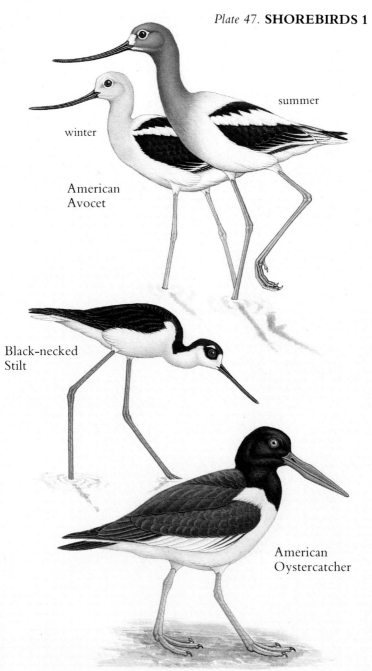

summer

winter

American
Avocet

Black-necked
Stilt

American
Oystercatcher

Plate 48. **SHOREBIRDS 2**

PIPING PLOVER 7"

Field Marks: One black breast band (sometimes incomplete); pale brown above, white below; yellow bill with black tip; yellowish legs. **Habitat:** Ocean beaches, sand flats, sandy lake and river shores. **Seasons:** Spring, summer, fall in North; fall, winter, spring in South. **Range:** S. Canada to Florida and Gulf of Mexico; winters on Atlantic and Gulf Coasts from Carolinas to Florida and Texas.

KILLDEER 10"

Field Marks: Two black breast bands; brown above, white below; tawny-orange rump evident in flight. **Habitat:** Short grassy and plowed fields; airports and golf courses; lake and river shores. **Seasons:** All year, but rare in winter northward, especially inland. **Range:** Canada to Florida and Gulf of Mexico. **Note:** This noisy bird has a loud, plaintive call, descriptive of its name.

SEMIPALMATED PLOVER 7"

Field Marks: One black breast band; dark brown above, white below; yellow bill with black tip; yellow legs. **Habitat:** Mud flats, beaches, lake and river shores. **Seasons:** Spring, summer, fall northward; fall, winter, spring in South. **Range:** Canada to Florida and Gulf of Mexico; winters chiefly on coast north to Carolinas.

RUDDY TURNSTONE 9"

Field Marks: Spring/summer—striking black, white, and reddish plumage; orange legs; fall/winter—much duller, generally brownish above, white below. **Habitat:** Rocky shores and islands, pebbly beaches, tidal flats, salt meadows. **Seasons:** Spring, summer, fall in North; fall, winter, spring in South. **Range:** Canada to Gulf of Mexico; winters chiefly along coasts of s. states north to Long Island; migrates along coast and also through interior via Great Lakes.

BLACK-BELLIED PLOVER 12"

Field Marks: Spring/summer—black below, mottled gray and white above, white forehead, and white behind eye and down neck; fall/winter—whitish below; white rump in flight. **Habitat:** Tidal flats, salt meadows, shores, plowed fields, large lawns, golf courses. **Seasons:** Spring, summer, fall in North; fall, winter, spring in South. **Range:** Canada to Florida and Gulf of Mexico; winters on Atlantic Coast north to Long Island.

Plate 48. **SHOR**

Piping Plover

Semipalmat
Plover

Killdeer

Ruddy
Turnstone

winter

summer

summer

winter

Black-bellied
Plover

Plate 49. **SHOREBIRDS 3**

WHIMBREL 17"

Field Marks: Long, decurved bill; brown and white head stripes; gray-brown body. **Habitat:** Shores, flats, prairies, salt meadows. **Seasons:** Chiefly spring and fall; winter in Deep South. **Range:** Canada to Florida and Gulf of Mexico; winters along Gulf and s. Atlantic Coasts, north to South Carolina.

MARBLED GODWIT 18"

Field Marks: Long bill, slightly upturned; tawny-brown body. **Habitat:** Prairies, pools, lake shores, coastal mud flats. **Seasons:** Chiefly spring inland, fall coastal; winters on southern coasts. **Range:** Canada to Florida and Gulf of Mexico, mainly coastal; winters along Atlantic and Gulf Coasts, chiefly from South Carolina to Florida and also Texas.

GREATER YELLOWLEGS 14"

Field Marks: Bright yellow legs; long bill; white rump in flight. **Habitat:** Tidal flats, marshes, lake and river shores, flooded fields, golf courses. **Seasons:** Spring and fall in most places; winter also in warmer regions. **Range:** Canada to Florida and Gulf of Mexico; winters in Deep South and along coast north to Long Island. **Note:** Bobs up and down.

WILLET 15"

Field Marks: Flashy black-and-white wings in flight; bluish gray legs; spring/summer—speckled; fall/winter—pale gray, unmarked. **Habitat:** Marshes, meadows, tidal flats, beaches. **Seasons:** All year in South; spring, summer, fall northward. **Range:** In East mainly coastal, breeding from Long Island to Florida and Texas; local north to Nova Scotia; winters chiefly from Virginia southward.

SHORT-BILLED DOWITCHER 11"

Field Marks: Very long bill; spring/summer—rusty-red breast with black spots; fall/winter—dull gray with white eye stripe; white rump wedge in flight. **Habitat:** Tidal flats, muddy shores, open marshes, grassy pools. **Seasons:** Spring, fall in most areas; also winter in South. **Range:** Canada to Florida and Gulf of Mexico; winters chiefly on coast north to Virginia.

Plate 49. **SHOREBIRDS 3**

Whimbrel

Marbled Godwit

Greater
Yellowlegs

winter

Willet
summer

Short-billed
Dowitcher
winter

Short-billed
Dowitcher
summer

119

Plate 50. **SHOREBIRDS 4**

UPLAND SANDPIPER 12"

Field Marks: Tawny-brown; thin neck; long tail; yellowish legs. **Habitat:** Short-grass prairies, hayfields, meadows, pastures. **Seasons:** Spring, summer, early fall. **Range:** Breeds in s. Canada and n. and c. U.S.; migrates throughout, but most numerous inland. **Note:** Often perches on poles and fence posts.

SPOTTED SANDPIPER 7½"

Field Marks: Spring/summer—black spots below; fall/winter—plain white below; white wedge at front of wing; rear end teeters up and down; in flight, flutters stiffly held, downcurved wings. **Habitat:** Shore of ponds and streams, often frequenting logs and rocks; beaches and dunes. **Seasons:** Spring, summer, fall in North; fall, winter, spring southward. **Range:** Canada to Florida and Gulf of Mexico; breeds south to c. U.S.; winters chiefly along Atlantic and Gulf Coasts from South Carolina to Texas.

SOLITARY SANDPIPER 8½"

Field Marks: Dark back and wings; white eye ring; dark green legs; barred black-and-white tail evident in flight. **Habitat:** Freshwater swamps and marshes; wooded ponds and streams. **Seasons:** Spring, late summer, fall. **Range:** Canada to Florida and Gulf of Mexico; more numerous inland than on coast. **Note:** Bobs up and down.

AMERICAN WOODCOCK 11"

Field Marks: Chunky; extremely long bill; "dead leaf" pattern above, cinnamon brown below. **Habitat:** Damp thickets near fields and pastures; under shrubs in parks and suburban yards during migration. **Seasons:** Spring, summer, fall over much of range; winter in South. **Range:** Breeds from s. Canada to Gulf states; winters chiefly in South, sometimes north along coast to s. New England.

COMMON SNIPE 11"

Field Marks: Extremely long bill; striped head and back; tawny-orange tail evident in flight. **Habitat:** Bogs, marshes, flooded fields, and meadows. **Seasons:** Spring, summer, fall in North; fall winter, spring in South. **Range:** Breeds from Canada to n. U.S.; winters in c. and s. U.S., north along Atlantic Coast to s. New England.

Plate 50. **SHOREBIRDS 4**

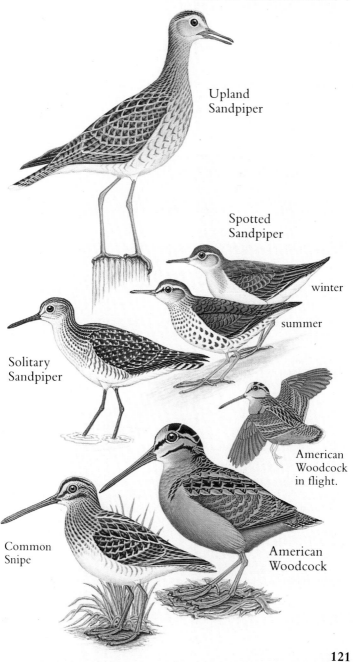

Upland Sandpiper

Spotted Sandpiper

winter

summer

Solitary Sandpiper

American Woodcock in flight.

Common Snipe

American Woodcock

Plate 51. **SHOREBIRDS 5**

RED KNOT 10½"

Field Marks: Spring/summer—brick red below; greenish legs; fall/winter—gray above, whitish below. Habitat: Tidal flats, salt meadows, lake shores. Seasons: Fall, winter, spring in South; spring, fall northward. Range: Canada to Florida and Gulf of Mexico; migrates chiefly along coast, but also via Great Lakes; winters on Gulf and Atlantic Coasts north to Long Island.

DUNLIN 8½"

Field Marks: Spring/summer—black patch on belly; reddish back; bill droops at tip; fall/winter—grayish-brown above, whitish below. Habitat: Tidal flats, lake shores, outer beaches. Seasons: Fall, winter, spring on coast; spring, fall inland. Range: Canada to Florida and Gulf of Mexico; winters on coast north to s. New England.

PURPLE SANDPIPER 8½"

Field Marks: Dark bill with pale base; yellow legs; white eye ring. Habitat: Rocky seacoasts and islands; jetties and breakwaters. Seasons: Fall, winter, spring, but most numerous in cold weather. Range: Winters along Atlantic Coast from s. Canada to North Carolina; rare on Great Lakes. Note: Our darkest sandpiper.

SANDERLING 7½"

Field Marks: Fall/winter—our palest sandpiper; spring/summer—rusty head, back, and breast. Habitat: Ocean beaches, sand flats, lake shores. Seasons: All year on coasts; spring, fall inland. Range: Canada to Florida and Gulf of Mexico; migrates through interior and along coast where it winters north to Maine. Note: Frequents ocean beaches, running in and out of waves.

SEMIPALMATED SANDPIPER 6"

Field Marks: Grayish above; blackish legs. Habitat: Mud flats, beaches, bare shores. Seasons: Chiefly spring, summer, fall. Range: Canada to Florida and Gulf of Mexico.

LEAST SANDPIPER 6"

Field Marks: Brownish above; heavily streaked breast; greenish yellow legs. Habitat: Grassy mud flats and pools; marshy edges. Seasons: Spring, summer, fall in North; fall, winter, spring in South. Range: Canada to Florida and Gulf of Mexico; winters mainly in coastal regions of South, rarely north to Virginia.

PECTORAL SANDPIPER 9"

Field Marks: Brownish above; heavily streaked breast, ending abruptly at white belly; yellowish legs. Habitat: Grassy pools and flats; flooded fields and golf courses; marsh edges. Seasons: Chiefly spring and fall. Range: Migrates through Canada and U.S., mainly interior in spring, along coast in fall.

Plate 51. **SHOREBIRDS 5**

Red Knot

winter

summer

winter

Dunlin

summer

Purple
Sandpiper

Sanderling

winter

summer

Semipalmated
Sandpiper

Pectoral
Sandpiper

Least
Sandpiper

Plate 52. **GULLS**

BONAPARTE'S GULL 13"

Field Marks: Pale gray wing with white wedge near tip; slender black bill; red legs; spring/summer—black head; fall/winter-white head with dark spot behind eye. **Habitat:** Ocean, bays, lakes, rivers. **Seasons:** Fall, winter, spring; summer also in Canada. **Range:** Canada to Florida and Gulf of Mexico.

LAUGHING GULL 16"

Field Marks: Dark gray back and wings; spring/summer—black head, dark red bill; fall/winter—white head mottled with gray, black bill. **Habitat:** Coastal—ocean beaches, bays, tidal flats, salt marshes, ponds, estuaries. **Seasons:** All year in South; spring, summer, fall in North. **Range:** Atlantic and Gulf Coasts from Maine to Texas; winters north to Virginia. **Note:** Call sounds like laughter—a strident "ha-ha-ha."

GREAT BLACK-BACKED GULL 29"

Field Marks: Black back and wings; yellow bill with red spot; pinkish legs. **Habitat:** Ocean beaches, tidal flats, bays, large lakes. **Seasons:** All year; winter in South. **Range:** Breeds on Atlantic Coast from Canada to Virginia; winters in South, rarely to Florida; uncommon and local on Great Lakes.

HERRING GULL 24"

Field Marks: Pale gray back and wings; yellow bill with red spot; pinkish legs. **Habitat:** Ocean beaches, lakes, rivers, harbors, fish piers, garbage dumps, flooded fields, golf courses, farms. **Seasons:** All year. **Range:** Chiefly on coast from Canada to North Carolina; less numerous inland, mainly on larger lakes; winters south to Gulf of Mexico. **Note:** This is *the* common large gull, often called "seagull" by the neophyte.

RING-BILLED GULL 19"

Field Marks: Pale gray back and wings; yellow bill with black band; yellow legs. **Habitat:** Lakes, rivers, beaches, bays, flooded and plowed fields, airports, golf courses, large lawns, refuse dumps. **Seasons:** All year in North, but scarce inland in winter; colder months in South. **Range:** Coasts and large lakes of s. Canada and n. U.S.; winters south to Florida and Gulf of Mexico, mainly along coast.

Plate 52. **GULLS**

Bonaparte's Gull

winter

summer

winter

Laughing
Gull

summer

Great
Black-backed
Gull

Herring Gull

juv.

adult

Ring-billed
Gull

Plate 53. **TERNS 1**

BLACK TERN 9½"

Field Marks: Black bill; spring/summer—black body, gray wings and tail; fall/winter—pied head, white below. **Habitat:** Inland marshes, lakes, ponds, sluggish rivers; fall—seacoasts, ocean. **Seasons:** Spring, summer, fall. **Range:** Breeds inland in Canada and n. U.S., south to Iowa, Illinois, Great Lakes, New York, New England; in fall migrates chiefly along coast.

LEAST TERN 9"

Field Marks: Spring/summer—yellow bill with black tip; yellow legs; white forehead; fall/winter—dark bill; white cap. **Habitat:** Ocean beaches, inlets, bays, sandbars in large rivers. **Seasons:** Spring, summer, early fall. **Range:** Atlantic and Gulf Coasts from Maine to Texas; large river systems from the Mississippi River and west through Louisiana, Arkansas, and Missouri.

COMMON TERN 14"

Field Marks: Spring/summer—red bill with black tip; fall/winter—dark bill, white forecrown; black nape. **Habitat:** Coastal—beaches, tidal flats, islands, ocean; inland—large lakes and rivers. **Seasons:** Spring, summer, fall in North; all year in South, but rare in summer. **Range:** Canada, both inland and coastal; U.S., chiefly along coast from Maine to North Carolina, also Great Lakes; winters on Atlantic and Gulf Coasts from South Carolina to Texas.

GULL-BILLED TERN 14"

Field Marks: Spring/summer—white plumage, black cap; short, thick, black bill; notched tail; fall/winter—white head. **Habitat:** Tidal flats, salt marshes, bays, lagoons; Florida—also inland marshes and lakes. **Seasons:** All year in s. Florida and along Gulf Coast; spring, summer, fall elsewhere. **Range:** Chiefly coastal, breeding locally on Gulf and Atlantic Coasts from Texas and Florida to s. New Jersey; winters from Florida Keys to Texas.

Plate 53. **TERNS 1**

winter

summer

Black Tern

summer

Least Tern

winter

winter

Common Tern

summer

Gull-billed Tern

summer

winter

127

Plate 54. **TERNS 2, SKIMMER**

SANDWICH TERN 17"

Field Marks: Black bill with yellow tip; spring/summer—black cap and crest; fall/winter—white forehead, black crest. **Habitat:** Sand beaches, inlets, bays, lagoons. **Seasons:** All year from Florida to Texas; spring, summer, fall from Virginia to Georgia. **Range:** Gulf Coast from Florida to Texas; less frequent on Atlantic Coast from Florida to Virginia. **Note:** Frequently associates with Royal Terns.

ROYAL TERN 19"

Field Marks: Orange bill; deeply forked tail; very pale flight feathers below; spring/summer—black cap and crest; fall/winter—white forehead, black crest. **Habitat:** Sand beaches, inlets, bays, lagoons. **Seasons:** All year in South; spring, summer, fall north of Carolinas. **Range:** Atlantic and Gulf Coasts from Maryland to Texas; north to Long Island in late summer and fall.

CASPIAN TERN 21"

Field Marks: Red bill; slightly forked tail; dark flight feathers below; spring/summer—black cap; fall/winter—mottled brown cap. **Habitat:** Large lakes and rivers, beaches, bays, coastal flats, lagoons. **Seasons:** All year in south; spring, summer, fall northward. **Range:** Canada to Florida and Gulf of Mexico; winters on s. Atlantic and Gulf Coasts from Carolinas to Texas.

BLACK SKIMMER 18"

Field Marks: Black above, white below; knifelike bill red at base, black at tip, upper portion much shorter than lower. **Habitat:** Ocean beaches, bays, estuaries, tidal flats; also large inland lakes in Florida. **Seasons:** All year from Carolinas to Texas; spring, summer, fall northward. **Range:** Atlantic and Gulf Coasts from Long Island to Texas.

Plate 54. **TERNS 2, SKIMMER**

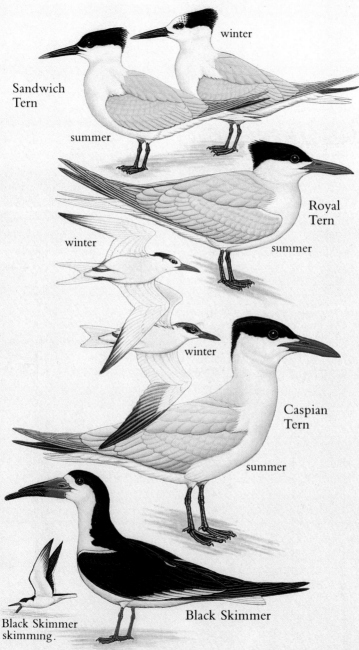

winter

Sandwich
Tern

summer

Royal
Tern

winter

winter

summer

Caspian
Tern

summer

Black Skimmer
skimming.

Black Skimmer

Further Comments
on the Plates

Plate 1—**Blue Birds**

The blue and white pattern and crest distinguish the Belted King-fisher and the Blue Jay from the other blue birds. The Kingfisher is heavier built than the Jay and is always found near water, while the Jay is a bird of woodland, park, and yard. The Kingfisher's crest is very large and bushy, the Jay's neater and smaller. The Eastern Bluebird lacks a crest and has a Robin-like reddish breast, so you should not mistake it for a Blue Jay. The larger size of the Blue Grosbeak distinguishes it from the otherwise similar-looking Indigo Bunting. The Bunting is all blue, whereas the Grosbeak has chestnut wing bars.

Plate 2—**Red Birds 1**

Some of our brightest birds are included here. The two tanagers are finch like and quite sluggish in action. The Scarlet Tanager can be distinguished from the Summer Tanager by its black wings and tail. The Northern Cardinal can be distinguished from the other red birds by its crest. The gaudy Painted Bunting has no rivals in coloration and is unmistakable. Moreover, the Bunting's range is limited to the south-central states and coastal sections of the Southeast.

Plate 3—**Red Birds 2**

The Redpoll is the smallest of this group and is easily identified by its black chin. It is seen only during the winter months. The House Finch is frequently confused with the Purple Finch, but the Purple Finch has more red and is a chunkier bird. The resident House Finch, introduced in the early 1940s from the West, is familiar and abundant. The easy-to-recognize Rose-breasted Grosbeak is conspicuous with its combination of red, black, and white.

Plate 4—**Black Birds 1**

The American Crow is among the largest of our perching birds and is therefore easy to spot. Unlike the smaller grackles, its tail is short. Close up, the Crow retains its all-black look, while the Common Grackle shows varying amounts of metallic or iridescent purplish and bronze coloring. The Grackle is also more streamlined than the bulky-looking Crow. The "caw" of the Crow is one of the most familiar bird sounds in rural and suburban areas. The tail of the much larger Boat-tailed Grackle is considerably longer than that of the Common Grackle. In addition, the Boat-tailed Grackle's range is more southerly, so it is very unlikely that you'll see it in New England.

Plate 5—Black Birds 2

The familiar European Starling is often mistaken for a grackle by beginners because of its generally dark color. However, it has a short tail compared to that of a grackle. Remember, Starlings have seasonal changes in plumage and bill color. The male Red-winged Blackbird is our only bird with a red and yellow shoulder patch, which makes it unmistakable. As for the Brown-headed Cowbird, its name tells the story: brown head, black body—there's no other bird like it.

Plate 6—Yellow Finches, Orioles

Black, yellow, and orange combinations mark the birds of this group, with the Baltimore Oriole being the most conspicuous. The bright orange color of this bird is a sight not easily forgotten. Where the Baltimore (Northern) Oriole is orange, the more southern Orchard Oriole is chestnut.

The large, attractive Evening Grosbeak and the much smaller, brightly colored American Goldfinch have much yellow in their plumage. They are frequent visitors at the feeding tray. The heavily streaked, sparrow like Pine Siskin is a close relative of both the Goldfinch and the Redpoll.

Plate 7—Open Country, Grassland Birds

This group consists of a miscellaneous assortment of predominantly unrelated brownish birds living in open grassland. The plumpness and short tail of the Eastern Meadowlark are distinctive, and the black V or chevron across the bright yellow breast makes it easy to identify.

The somewhat similar-looking but much smaller and unrelated Horned Lark occurs in large flocks in cold weather, as does the attractive and conspicuous Snow Bunting. The tail-wagging American (Water) Pipit occurs chiefly on migration. It is sparrow sized, but has a slender bill. The Bobolink is buff and brown in fall, but in spring the male is our only land bird that is black below and light above.

Plate 8—Brown Birds 1

This plate treats the wrens as one group, and the American Robin and Eastern (Rufous-sided) Towhee as another.

The small, restless wrens are chiefly brown in color and may be recognized by their frequent habit of cocking up their tails. The House Wren is found near buildings, as is the more southerly Carolina Wren, and the Marsh Wren inhabits cattail marshes.

The American Robin is one of our most familiar birds, often seen on lawns digging for worms. The male Eastern (Rufous-sided) Towhee can, at first glance, be mistaken for a Robin because of its reddish sides. The black back and white belly should make the difference apparent. The female Towhee is even more like the Robin, because it is brown above rather than black.

Plate 9—**Brown Birds 2**

The five species on this plate are either streaked (Brown Thrasher) or spotted (the remaining four). The Brown Thrasher, larger than the American Robin, has a long look about it. It is often mistaken for a thrush, but has a much longer tail and is streaked below rather than spotted.

As for the Wood Thrush and the Hermit Thrush, remember: Wood Thrush—reddish about the head and upper back; Hermit Thrush—reddish tail.

Although the Ovenbird and the Northern Waterthrush can be confused with each other, the former has an eye ring, the latter an eye stripe. Moreover, habitat is one of the keys to identification: The Ovenbird is mainly found in wooded areas; the Northern Waterthrush, as its name implies, is often associated with water. Although they both superficially resemble thrushes, they are not related to that family, but are ground-dwelling warblers.

Plate 10—**Sparrows 1**

This group includes predominantly brownish sparrowlike birds. The Dickcissel visits the eastern seaboard during the fall migration. It is occasionally found at feeders with the ubiquitous House Sparrow. The females of these two species closely resemble each other. The three sparrows shown here (Fox, Song, and Savannah) are streaked below and are thus distinguished from the sparrows on the next plate, which are unstreaked. The unrelated House Sparrow looks superficially like the other sparrows, but has a large black bib. Everyone should know this common bird.

The gray and white Dark-eyed Junco is also one of the sparrows and is therefore grouped with them, although at first glance it doesn't seem to belong.

Plate 11—**Sparrows 2**

The six brownish birds on this plate are all sparrows that are unstreaked below. You will notice that four of them have reddish or rusty caps. That narrows the choice down to the Swamp, Field, Tree, and Chipping Sparrows. It's a matter of learning how each rusty-capped bird differs in other respects. For example, the Tree Sparrow has a conspicuous black chest spot, the Field Sparrow a pinkish bill and an eye ring, the Chipping Sparrow black and white eye stripes, and the Swamp Sparrow a white throat that stands out against its dull gray breast. Both the White-crowned and the White-throated Sparrows possess diagnostic black-and-white head stripes, the former with a pinkish bill and gray throat and face, the latter with a gleaming white throat and a yellow spot in front of the eye.

Plate 12—**Large Grayish Birds**

The darkest of this group is the Gray Catbird, whose uniform slate colors makes it easy to identify. It is more secretive than the Northern Mockingbird and is usually found within thick shrubbery. The Mockingbird is, if anything, an exhibitionist, and is seen frequently on the most exposed perches imaginable—treetops, utility poles, and wires. The Mockingbird often pumps its tail when perched and flashes its wings, showing the large white patches. The Loggerhead Shrike superficially looks like the Mockingbird, but has a black facial mask and a shorter tail. It also has a thick, hooked bill and much black in the wings and tail. The Cedar Waxwing is rather tawny in tone, but with gray wings, rump, and tail. The sleek, velvety look of its feathers gives it a distinctive appearance, together with the fact that it is also crested.

Plate 13—**Small Grayish Birds**

The two greenish gray kinglets are nearly as small as hummingbirds. They are related to the Old World Warblers and are extremely active and restless, continually moving about. Both kinglets have prominent head markings, the Ruby-crown with an eye ring, the Golden-crown with an eye stripe. The Gnatcatcher is blue-gray with a very long tail. Superficially it looks like a tiny mockingbird. The grayish colored Tufted Titmouse and Black-capped Chickadee are two of our tamest birds, especially the latter. Both come readily to the well-stocked feeding station.

Plate 14—**Vireos**

Vireos are relatively sluggish, thick-billed birds, quite unlike the active, restless, slender-billed warblers, which they resemble superficially in their generally olive, yellow, and white coloring. They often perch in shrubbery or high in the trees among the foliage, and so may be difficult to find.

The red eye of the Red-eyed Vireo is not apparent at any distance, but the white eye stripe bordered by black makes it one of the easiest members of this family to identify. Notice particularly whether the bird has wing bars or not and whether it has an eye ring or eye stripe(s). Of the five vireos included, both the Red-eyed and the Warbling lack wing bars but have eye stripes. The remaining three species, however, possess both wing bars and eye rings. They are the White-eyed, Yellow-throated, and Blue-headed (Solitary) Vireos.

Plates 15 to 18—**Warblers**

A large family of active and, for the most part, brightly colored birds, mostly smaller than sparrows and with slender bills. The warblers are misnamed, because many of them do not warble at all, but instead have buzzy, insect like notes. Others, such as the Common Yellowthroat, have more distinctive and/or attractive songs.

As with most of the other birds in this volume, the plates show the warblers in their readily identifiable plumages, i.e., spring and summer males in breeding dress. Many that can be identified quickly in the spring are extremely difficult to identify in the fall, when they are relatively drab and otherwise quite similar in appearance, and consequently they are known as the "confusing fall warblers."

Most, but not all, warblers have some yellow in them. Several of these warblers are distinct enough to make identification relatively easy, and they are the group with which to start.

The Prothonotary Warbler, with the bright golden, almost orange, color in its head and breast, is unmistakable. Also very easy to identify is the male American Redstart, with its black and orange pattern. The Yellow Warbler's color is much less vivid, and the reddish streaks, although noticeable at close range, still leave the bird with an all-yellow look.

The black mask of the male Common Yellowthroat is another distinctive field mark The two warblers with "black-throated" in their names do indeed have black throats. The all-black face and throat of the Black-throated Blue Warbler is quite different from those of the Black-throated Green Warbler, whose throat is black but whose face is yellow.

The Magnolia Warbler and the Yellow-rumped (Myrtle) Warbler both have yellow rumps, but that of the Yellow-rumped is generally more visible, whereas the Magnolia has prominent white tail patches, which the Yellow-rumped lacks.

Three other warblers can be told apart quickly: Cape May, chestnut cheek patch; Bay-breasted, chestnut crown, throat, and sides; Chestnut-sided, the color on the sides.

What is true of these warblers is true of all of the warblers in this volume: Each species has one or two distinctive field marks that set it apart from all the others.

The following important questions about field marks should be answered when identifying warblers:

1. Does it have either wing bars or wing patches?
2. Does it lack these marks?
3. Is it streaked below?
4. Is it without streaks?
5. Is it yellow or mainly yellow below?
6. Is it white or mainly white below?
7. Does it have conspicuous black markings anywhere about the head, body, or tail?

Plates 19 and 20—**Tree Clingers and Woodpeckers**
The birds on these two plates spend much of their time on trees—woodpeckers, nuthatches, a creeper, and a warbler.

Nuthatches are often observed head down as they explore a tree for food—the White-breasted on the trunks and large branches; the Red-breasted on the smaller branches, especially on conifers, feeding among the cones. The Brown Creeper, on the other hand, is always seen spiraling up a tree, its dull brown back blending in with the bark. Its decurved bill distinctive. The Black-and-White Warbler's actions are more like those in the Brown Creeper, although it is usually not in an upright position. Its actions are quite unlike those of most other warblers, which feed in the foliage, not on tree trunks. The Black-and-White Warbler is distinguishable from the Blackpoll Warbler by its striped head.

Woodpeckers are most frequently seen in an upright stance on the trunk of a tree or a telephone pole as they climb in search of insects.

The exception is the familiar Northern Flicker, our only brown woodpecker, which often feeds on the ground, picking up ants.

Most woodpeckers have black-and-white patterns of some sort, either in patches or in stripes and bars, and they usually have some red on the head. Only the Red-headed Woodpecker has an entire red head, however. They range from the crow-size Pileated Woodpecker to the very small Downy Woodpecker. The Downy and Hairy Woodpeckers are replicas of each other, the Downy being the smaller and more numerous of the two. Other members of this group are the zebra-backed Red-bellied Woodpecker and the Yellow-bellied Sapsucker.

All of the birds on these two plates are hole nesters, with the exception of the Black and White Warbler, which lays its eggs on the ground.

Plate 21—**Flycatchers**

Flycatchers' behavior is unique: They fly out from a perch for an insect and almost invariably return to the same perch. The upright stance of these birds is also a good means of identification.

Some things to remember: The Great Crested Flycatcher is the only member of the family in our area with the combination of the yellow belly and rufous flashes in the wings and tail; the Eastern Kingbird has a white band across its tail tip; the localized Gray Kingbird of the southeastern coastal states has a much larger bill and a dark mask through the eye; the Eastern Phoebe is a tail wagger, but is often overlooked because it is so uniformly drab in color, as are the dull-colored Eastern Wood-Pewee and the Least Flycatcher.

Plate 22—**Swift, Swallows**

Swallows superficially look like swifts but are not related to them. Unlike swifts, which are drab, swallows are often attractively patterned and colored.

Although the swallows are generally thought of as having forked tails (the swallow-tailed coat), actually only the Barn Swallow's tail is forked deeply enough to be considered its principal field mark. In the others, the tail is either notched or, as in the Cliff Swallow, almost square. Swallows are extremely graceful on the wing. They are frequently observed perched on utility wires, often in huge flocks.

The Chimney Swift appears to have no tail at all. It is just an oblong, dark bird with long, pointed, scimitar-shaped wings, built for speed. Unlike swallows, swifts do not perch on wires or on bare twigs. They are seen together, however, in the air at times. Swifts are among the fastest flying of all birds, hence their name.

Plate 23—**Nightjars, Hummingbird**

These birds are never confused with each other. They are, however, grouped together because they are related, which is hard to believe.

Nighthawks, although chiefly nocturnal in habits, often are seen during the day feeding on nocturnal insects. Members of this family are mottled in subdued browns and grays, with prominent white patches in the wings and tail and on the throat. Whip-poor-wills are much more easily heard than seen. During migrations, however, they are flushed from the ground, occasionally in parks or even in one's yard.

Hummingbirds are tiny, brilliantly colored birds that have long, needlelike bills for probing flowers. They should not be confused with any other bird as they hover in the air with rapidly moving wings, like a large bee or moth.

Plate 24—**Cuckoo, Pigeons**

The Rock Pigeon, along with the House Sparrow and European Starling, is undoubtedly the bird most familiar to urban dwellers. It is also ubiquitous, occurring everywhere humans are found. Distinctive is the way the Pigeon's head bobs back and forth when it walks.

The Mourning Dove has a fawn-colored body. Its tail is long and pointed, unlike the Pigeon's, which is short and fan shaped. The tiny Common Ground-Dove of the southeast is barely larger than a sparrow. When it flies, it shows a bright rufous patch on each wing.

The slender, long-tailed profile of the Yellow-billed Cuckoo is similar to that of the Mourning Dove. However, the downcurved bill and the brown and white plumage are distinctive.

Plate 25—**Game Birds**

These birds are all chickenlike, with the Northern Bobwhite the smallest, the Wild Turkey the largest. Their plumage generally has a mottled brown appearance, although both the Turkey and the Ring-Necked Pheasant have brightly colored facial wattles in the males. The white neck ring of the Pheasant is enough for identification, but if you miss that, the very long tail will leave you in no doubt. The Ruffed Grouse, a chicken-sized bird, is the fourth member of this group.

Plates 26 to 29—**Hawks**

With this group, we come to the diurnal (daytime) birds of prey—hawks, eagles, falcons, kites, and vultures—all of which eat animal matter, including mammals, birds, reptiles, fish, insects, and carrion; the last are relished by the two vultures, which are useful scavengers.

The most important clue in the identification of hawks is the shape of the wings and tail, especially noticeable in overhead flight; distinctive is the manner of flight, as are the patterns and colors. The plates and accompanying text emphasize these features. Only adults are illustrated, unless otherwise noted.

Hawks vary in size as well as in shape, the American Kestrel (Sparrow Hawk) being about 10 inches or so, the Bald Eagle well over 3 feet. Females are larger than males, except for the two vultures, which are of equal size.

Most of our hawks are generally fairly widespread in distribution, whereas the Black Vulture and the Swallow-tailed Kite are confined to the southern portions of our area. The pointed wings and long, forked tail of the graceful and handsome Kite make it easy to recognize in flight. One hawk that is relatively easy to identify is the Northern Harrier (Marsh Hawk), often seen flying low over marshes or fields looking for prey. The white rump is very visible and a sure clue to its identity. The conspicuous black-and-white Osprey, once in grave danger from pesticides, has made a strong recovery. It is sometimes seen diving for fish—feet first. Our national emblem, the Bald Eagle, if in adult plumage, is easily recognized by its gleaming white head and tail.

Plates 30 and 31—**Owls**

Owls are chiefly nocturnal birds of prey, although three open-country owls are mainly diurnal—the Snowy, Short-eared, and Burrowing. All are active chiefly on overcast days. All owls have large heads and appear to be neckless. Some, like the Eastern Screech-Owl and the Great Horned Owl, have red and gray color phases. Most of our owls have light-colored eyes, which give them a somewhat fierce expression; only the Barn and Barred are dark-eyed, imparting a mild appearance.

Plate 30 contains five kinds of woodland owls: Great Horned, Barred, Long-eared, Screech, and Saw-whet; Plate 31 has four open-country owls: Barn, Snowy, Short-eared, and Burrowing.

Owls' very large eyes are an adaptation for night hunting, and their hearing is also very keen. The head tufts present on some "eared" and "horned" owls are strictly ornamental and are used for neither hearing nor fighting.

Owls range greatly in size, from the Great Horned, which is as large as a Red-tailed Hawk—both more than 2 feet in length—to the diminutive Saw-whet Owl, smaller than a Robin. The little Saw-whet is ordinarily extremely tame, allowing the observer an unusually close approach, to within a few feet.

Plate 32—Geese, Swans

There are many white birds, but in our part of the world few are as large as a swan. The Mute Swan, about 60 inches in length, is one of the largest birds you are likely to see in the United States or Canada. Because it is such a familiar emblem in literature, art, and legend, a close look at the plate should be sufficient to fix it in your mind and to differentiate it from other large white birds you may see in or near the water. There are some things to look for, however. It is about twice the size of the Snow Goose. Aside from the Snow Goose, the other geese included in this guide are dark bodied, and therefore unlikely to be confused with the Snow Goose. The biggest problem for a beginner is distinguishing the geese from the ducks. As a rule, geese have longer necks than ducks (just as swans differ from geese). Geese are generally larger, and their bodies are heavier. Furthermore, there are no all-white ducks (except the domesticated Pekin Duck), although one of the most abundant geese, the Snow Goose, is almost all white, and therefore rather easy to identify once you've decided that it's not a swan or the partly white Muscovy (barnyard) Duck. The so-called Blue Goose, though, is a little trickier, as the plate makes clear.

In our area, the two other common geese are also rather easily identified. The Canada Goose is a big bird (the largest goose in the world)—much larger than any duck—and the long black neck with the white chin strap makes it unmistakable. The Brant is less distinctive, but it is much smaller and darker than the Canada Goose—about the size of the Mallard; there is no chin strap, just a suggestion of a white neck spot.

Geese are frequently seen grazing on land, much more often than swans and most ducks.

Plates 33 to 37—**Ducks**

For many birders, ducks are among the most confusing of waterbirds, except perhaps for sandpipers. For one thing, ducks are often a long distance off and difficult to see clearly, even with binoculars. For another, many are frustratingly similar in appearance, even close-up.

As you go through the plates, you'll notice that ducks may be grouped as follows:

Plates 33-34—Tipping Ducks. These ducks feed by tipping and upending on or near the surface of the water; they also feed on land.

Plates 35-37—Diving Ducks. These ducks feed by diving from the surface, sometimes deeply.

As for color differences, ducks may also be grouped according to whether their heads are all or mostly green—the Mallard, Northern Shoveler, and both Common and Red-breasted Mergansers have all-green heads. Within this group there are also marked differences: The Mallard has a white ring around the neck, the Shoveler a spoon-shaped bill, one of the two mergansers is crested, and both have long red bills. One might also categorize ducks by various white patches on the head, wings, or body. Many have prominent white mark-ings—Northern Pintail, the American Widgeon (Baldpate), Blue-winged Teal, Surf Scoter, Oldsquaw, Common Eider, Common Goldeneye, Bufflehead, Ruddy Duck, and all three mergansers.

Most ducks are difficult to identify in flight except after experi-ence. For this reason, the illustrations show them only on water or land, where one has the best opportunity of identifying them.

The generally duller females are depicted with the males because they are often seen together.

The Mallard is our most familiar duck. In spring, in Florida and along the Gulf Coast west to Louisiana and Texas, the Mallard departs for its northern breeding grounds. Still present, however, is the similar-looking Mottled Duck—a close relative—in which both sexes look like the female Mallard, but with the head and neck buff or tan.

The Ring-necked Duck is poorly named, as the chestnut ring at the base of the neck is very inconspicuous and almost never seen. Hunters use the name "Ring-billed Duck," which is much more apt.

The handsome Hooded Merganser, like the Goldeneye, Buffle-head, and Wood Duck, nests in tree cavities in wooded swamps, and sometimes in nest boxes.

Plate 38—**Rails, Coot, Gallinules**
Coots and gallinules are ducklike birds with chickenlike bills. The white bill contrasting with the dark gray body is a sure sign of the American Coot, and the red bills shown on the plate are essential for identification of the Common Moorhen (Common Gallinule) and Purple Gallinule. The two rails are chickenlike in shape, with slender, decurved bills. They live in marshes and are sometimes difficult to see.

Plate 39—**Grebes**
Grebes, loonlike with lobed feet, sit low in the water, appear to be tailless, and have daggerlike bills. They are therefore easily distinguished from ducks. The Pied-billed Grebe, however, has a thick, chickenlike bill. All grebes, when diving from the surface, sink into the water and reappear at another spot.

Plate 40—**Guillemot, Loons**
Loons are black-and-white goose-sized divers with short, thick necks and sharp, pointed bills. On the water, loons can be told from cormorants by the position of their bills, which point straight ahead instead of slanting upward.

The Black Guillemot is a member of the family called alcids—black-and-white ducklike seabirds with pointed bills. This family includes auks, murres, guillemots, and puffins, among others. The very large white-wing patch of the Black Guillemot easily distinguishes it from loons and grebes.

Plate 41—**Cormorants, Anhinga**
The three species of cormorants in our area are large, black, goose-like birds in flight, but more loonlike when on water. They have hooked bills. When perched they stand erect, often with their wings spread out to dry. Unlike other birds, cormorants and the Anhinga do not have waterproof feathers because they lack oil glands.

The Anhinga is a large, cormorant-like bird. It has a sharp, pointed bill for spearing fish and a thin, snakelike neck, which gives the bird its popular name of "Snakebird." It swims with the body submerged and only the head and neck out of water. Like cormorants, these birds spread out their wings to dry. Anhingas, in flight, flap and glide and often soar high in the air circling around like storks.

Double-crested Cormorants are the most numerous and wide-spread members of the family and, in migration, are frequently seen flying overhead with steady wingbeats in very large numbers, either in long lines or in V-shaped flocks. Unlike geese, however, they are silent.

Plate 42—Gannet, Pelicans, Frigatebird

The pelicans, of which there are two kinds in our area, are familiar to all. One—the White Pelican—is mainly inhabitant of inland fresh waters, although it spends the winter months along the coasts from Florida to Texas. The other—the Brown Pelican—lives near the ocean along the beaches. Lines of these birds flap and sail in unison low over the waves. They plunge from moderate heights into the sea for fish and often perch on posts, piers, and fishing boats. Unlike the Brown Pelican, the White Pelican fishes from the surface in shallow waters. In flight, these spectacular birds also alternately flap and glide in unison, sometimes in large flocks.

The Magnificent Frigatebird is mainly tropical. These birds are wonderful flyers, seeming to float effortlessly in the air for long periods. They rob other seabirds of their catch, forcing them to drop or disgorge their fish. They may also be observed at close range around the piers at Miami, following fishing boats.

The Gannet is our sole representative of the mainly warm-water boobies and may be observed off our beaches, especially during stormy weather or when strong winds send them in close to shore. Gannets fly with stiff wingbeats, flapping or sailing, depending on the wind. These spectacular birds are unmistakable as they plunge from great heights into the sea after fish.

Plates 43 to 45—Herons, Cranes

Herons are wading birds whose habitat is often the best clue to their identification. They can usually be seen picking their way slowly through shallow water in the marshes (the two bitterns) or along the mudflats searching for fish, frogs, crustaceans, and other aquatic forms of life. They may also be observed roosting together in large numbers in trees and bushes near water where they breed. They may have either long or short legs and long or short necks, but they all have long bills, except for the field-inhabiting, insect-eating Cattle Egret and the Night-Herons.

The various white forms known as egrets, of which there are four species in our area, are members of this family (Great, Reddish, Snowy, and Cattle Egrets). People often confuse egrets and herons. All egrets are herons, but the reverse is not true—all herons are *not* egrets.

As for the Cattle Egret, this immigrant from Africa has spread far and wide and has become established over much of the United States. Cattle Egrets feed on the various insects that are flushed from the grass by moving cattle, other livestock, and even farm tractors.

The Little Blue Heron occurs in two or more color forms, depending on its age. A mixed blue-white (pied) phase also occurs and is especially prevalent in the South.

Unlike other herons, the American Bittern is solitary and reluctant to fly. For safety it relies on protective coloration; if it stands motionless, its streaked breast blends in with the reeds.

Although often skulking in the reeds, the Least Bittern may be seen in short flights, skimming over the top of the marsh or occasionally observed grasping the cattails and even climbing among them.

Many people mistake herons for cranes. Cranes differ from the unrelated herons, particularly when in flight. Unlike herons, cranes fly with necks outstretched in a V formation, or in long lines, like geese; they also flap and glide. Herons, on the other hand, fly with necks kinked or folded in, with slow, steady wingbeats in loose flocks. The one crane in our area is called the gray-colored Sandhill Crane.

Plate 46—**Stork, Ibises, Spoonbill, Limpkin**

Except for the Glossy Ibis, the birds shown on this plate are found only in the southern portion of our area. Although the Wood Stork and the "Great White" Heron are both white and about same size, the dark head and neck of the Wood Stork should make identification easy. Moreover, the Stork has much black in the wings, whereas the Heron is all white. As for both the Glossy and White Ibises, as well as the Limpkin, the slender decurved bills of these birds separate them from the others on this page. The flattened, shovel-shaped bill of the pink and white Roseate Spoonbill should make it easy to distinguish from the all-pink Flamingo, which is not included in this book because it does not occur naturally in our area. Spoonbills move their heads from side to side as they feed in shallow water. The highly specialized Limpkin feeds almost exclusively on freshwater snails.

The birds on this plate fly with outstretched necks, flap, and glide. These birds should not be confused with the Sandhill Crane, which is gray, or with the herons, which fly with folded necks.

Plates 47 to 51—**Shorebirds**

The shorebirds or "waders," as they are sometimes called, frequent the shores of lakes and rivers and the edges of marshes, as well as tidal flats and ocean beaches. They reflect a diversity of types, which are matched by their many different names. There are two major subdivisions, based primarily on bill shapes, which are adaptations for feeding: (1) the plovers, with short, stubby bills, and (2) the sandpipers and allies, with long, slender bills. In addition, the following names are utilized in this very large and varied group: oystercatcher, stilt, avocet, godwit, curlew, whimbrel, willet, yellowlegs, dowitcher, knot, turnstone, woodcock, snipe, and dunlin.

One of the first things to look for in a shorebird is the length and shape of the bill. For instance, oystercatchers have laterally compressed, knifelike bills for opening up shellfish; avocets and godwits have upturned bills; curlews and whimbrels have downturned ones; dowitchers, snipes, and woodcocks have long, straight, slender bills for probing deep into the mud and ooze; stilts, yellowlegs, willets, and many sandpipers have long, needlelike bills for feeding in deep water and for picking up animal life directly from the ground or on shallow pools and mudflats.

Plates 52 to 54—**Gulls, Terns, Skimmer**
The most common and familiar whitish or grayish birds seen flying at the seashore or near lakes and other bodies of water are the gulls. Several features distinguish gulls from terns, in general. Gulls are usually, but not always, larger than terns. Gull bills are heavier than those of terns and are hooked, whereas those of terns are pointed. Terns usually keep their bills pointed downward in flight, while gulls keep theirs pointed straight ahead. Most terns dive headfirst into the water for food, while gulls pick up their food from the surface. Terns generally are more graceful looking, especially on the wing. Many species have forked tails. Most gulls are mottled with gray and white (even brownish in young birds), whereas terns are usually white with some kind of black cap or crest.

The unique Black Skimmer, with its unequal upper and lower mandibles, is especially easy to identify when it feeds on the wing, its bill skimming the surface of the water. These striking birds never fail to impress even the most blasé observer.

Attracting Birds

As the sport and hobby of birding have grown over the years, so too has the use of bird feeders. They not only bring more species to the backyard but they also help the birds themselves, especially in colder areas where snow and ice may cover up their food. In retrospect, it can be seen that feeders were an important factor in the rapid spread of some species (for example, the Northern Cardinal) to areas where they had been rare or even unknown. As conservation became of widespread interest to millions, so too did increased awareness of the need to protect and aid birds. As a result, setting out feeders and gardening with an eye to attracting birds have become national pastimes. It is obvious that the greater the variety of birds, the greater the enjoyment of backyard birding.

Getting actively involved in feeding birds requires selecting feeders, setting them up in the right locations, and filling them with a good mixture of food.

Feeders

Feeders may be purchased in hardware stores, garden centers, nurseries, pet shops, and supermarkets. They range from simple feeders to elaborate bird "cafeterias." They can even be built by the unhandiest birder. In selecting a feeder, remember that all you want is something to hold the food; it does not have to be complicated. Avoid metal feeders which heat up in the summer sun and become tacky in freezing weather.

Feeders can be easily fashioned out of common objects found around the house. A plastic bleach bottle, for example, can be converted into a feeder, as can milk cartons, shoe boxes, and small wooden crates. Containers in which doors and windows have been cut can be suspended from a tree with metal coat hangers. A flat board with a raised edge around it to keep the seeds from spilling over also makes an efficient feeder. A shallow candy box on the bedroom windowsill can serve as an alarm clock, as chirping birds are quite regular when clamoring for food early in the morning.

Store-bought feeders come in all sizes, shapes, and materials.

Some are made of redwood and have glass sides and a shelf for food. Others look like plastic bubbles, and can be hung up almost anywhere. There are also seed silos, post feeders, hummingbird feeders, and even small transparent boxes that can be attached to the windowpane with a suction cup. Many feeders dole out the seeds a little at a time, avoiding spillage and protecting the food from inclement weather.

We have just been talking about feeders used primarily for seed. Feeder use is not confined to seed eaters, however. Many also have suet racks for insect-eating birds, such as woodpeckers. Mesh bags (the kind that hold onions and oranges) may be filled with chunks of suet and suspended from a hook or branch. Be sure that the bags swing freely, otherwise aggressive Starlings, which don't like the motion, will take over. The suet and fat should be discontinued in warm weather, because they melt or become rancid.

Nectar-feeding birds such as hummingbirds will frequent such flowers as trumpet vine, red petunias, salvia, or jewelweed. Hummers are especially attracted to red and orange colors. A hummingbird feeder filled with sugar-water and a little red tape or paint on the bottle is another way to lure these birds into your yard.

Before putting a feeder into operation, be sure that its location is right. The ideal place is out of the wind, near natural cover, in an area that is sunny in winter and shady in summer. A kitchen window is frequently the perfect place. The ability to see the feeder from the house is the first prerequisite. Next, you want to see the *birds* in it, not squirrels. The feeder should be set up where squirrels cannot decimate the food supply and where cats cannot decimate the bird supply. Squirrels are very acrobatic. Consequently, baffles above and below feeders are necessary to keep them out, and the feeders must be away from trees and bushes so that the squirrels cannot leap into them. Once the station is working, food should not be placed on the ground, where a preoccupied bird can become easy prey of a cat. This is not to say that birds, on their own, won't feed on the ground; many do, but at least you won't be responsible for any mishap that might occur. To keep Rock Pigeons away, enclosures can be made with wire mesh large enough for small birds but too small for Rock Pigeons.

Now that the feeder is ready, what kind of seed should you get? Many commercial mixes of wild bird feed include large amounts of milo (round red seeds) or buckwheat, oats, and wheat, all of which you will find left behind in the feeder. Your best bet is sunflower seed, the favorite of Cardinals, grosbeaks, chickadees, House Finches, and Blue Jays. For smaller seed-eating birds, white and red millet and cracked corn are popular. A number of birds favor peanut hearts, but this feed is also very attractive to Starlings, which can quickly become pests. If you would like to try for Goldfinches, Pine Siskins, and Purple Finches, thistle seed (also called niger seed) is sure to do the trick.

Many table scraps are also good for enticing birds, as are stale dry cereals, doughnuts, crackers and bread (especially favored by blackbirds), and fruit—grapes, cherries, apples, oranges, and bananas for Mockingbirds and orioles. Near the shore and at ponds, bread will be gobbled up by gulls and ducks.

After choosing a feeder (or more than one, to attract a larger variety of birds), you must decide when to start using it. Wintertime in the North is the essential period for feeding birds; do not stop until mild weather sets in.

It takes time to establish a feeder. You have to be patient and wait for birds to discover it. Unless birds are hard pressed for food, they are as likely to go beetle grubbing or seed gathering in an empty lot as to visit a feeder. Bad weather and a shortage of food will bring them to you. An easily available supply of their favorite foods, however, can lure them away from their usual feeding habits. The variety of birds that come to feeders will depend on the variety of food put out. In warmer regions, the feeding station is more fun for the birder than a necessity for the birds. In colder areas, you must keep in mind that once a feeding station has been established in the fall, many birds become dependent on it. So don't start a feeding program if you are going to be away in the midwinter months and will be leaving the feeder untended.

Once the feeding routine has become established, birds will continue as steady customers until it is suspended in the spring, when buds, berries, and bugs are plentiful. At this time, put out some yarn, cotton, and strips of paper for nest-building birds.

If feeding is prolonged into the summer, adult birds may bring their young to the feeder, and eventually the young will come by themselves. Remember that young birds are unwary and easily caught by cats. If you continue to feed birds, you must make sure that cats don't come for a free meal too. To keep cats from pouncing out of the shrubs, a low metal or chicken-wire fence should be installed at the edge of flower borders, particularly thick borders (lily and iris beds), which are favorite hideouts for cats.

Birds Attracted by Food Type

	Seeds	Suet	Nectar	Grasses, Fruiting Shrubs and Trees
American Crow	●	●		●
American Goldfinch	●			●
American Robin				●
Baltimore (Northern) Oriole			●	●
Black-capped Chickadee	●	●		●
Blue Grosbeak				●
Blue Jay	●	●		●
Blue-headed (Solitary) Vireo				●
Boat-tailed Grackle	●			●
Brown Creeper		●		●
Brown Thrasher		●		●
Brown-headed Cowbird	●			●
Carolina Wren	●	●		●
Cedar Waxwing				●
Chipping Sparrow	●			●
Common Grackle	●			●
Common Ground-Dove	●			●
Common Redpoll	●			●
Common Yellowthroat				●
Dark-eyed Junco	●			●
Dickcissel	●			●
Downy Woodpecker	●	●		●
Eastern Bluebird				●
Eastern Phoebe				●
Eastern (Rufous-sided) Towhee	●			●
European Starling	●	●		●
Evening Grosbeak	●	●		●
Field Sparrow	●			
Fox Sparrow	●	●		
Gray Catbird	●	●		●
Hairy Woodpecker	●	●		●
Hermit Thrush				●
House Finch	●			●

	Seeds	Suet	Nectar	Grasses, Fruiting Shrubs and Trees
House Sparrow	•			•
House Wren		•		•
Indigo Bunting	•			•
Mourning Dove	•			•
Northern Bobwhite	•			•
Northern Cardinal	•			•
Northern Flicker		•		•
Northern Mockingbird	•	•		•
Orchard Oriole			•	•
Painted Bunting	•			•
Pileated Woodpecker	•	•		•
Pine Siskin	•			•
Purple Finch	•			•
Red-bellied Woodpecker	•	•		•
Red-breasted Nuthatch	•	•		•
Red-eyed Vireo				•
Red-headed Woodpecker	•	•		•
Red-winged Blackbird	•			•
Ring-necked Pheasant	•			•
Rock (Dove) Pigeon	•			•
Rose-breasted Grosbeak	•			•
Ruby-crowned Kinglet		•		
Ruby-throated Hummingbird			•	•
Scarlet Tanager			•	•
Song Sparrow	•			•
Summer Tanager			•	•
Tree Sparrow	•			•
Tufted Titmouse	•	•		•
White-breasted Nuthatch	•	•		•
White-crowned Sparrow	•			•
White-throated Sparrow	•			•
Wild Turkey	•			•
Wood Thrush				•
Yellow-billed Cuckoo				•

Water

Water is as much a part of a feeding station as food. Winter and summer, birds need drinking water. Some birds will also bathe, even on bitterly cold days. Heating mechanisms may be installed in birdbaths to keep them from freezing. In summer, on hot dry days, an oscillating lawn sprinkler will bring birds down from the treetops—small birds, such as warblers and kinglets, that you never suspected were around will turn up. An old leaking bucket filled with water and dripping into a pan will serve the same purpose.

Nest Boxes

In addition to creating a sanctuary for birds with feeders, birdbaths, and food, nest boxes can be provided for breeding birds. In Bluebird country, for example, there is intense competition between other hole-nesting birds and the shy native Bluebird, which gives way to aggressive European Starlings and House Sparrows. Entrance holes should be small enough for the Bluebird alone. Tree Swallows might move into a Bluebird house, but they are welcome guests. Just put out more houses, and there will be plenty of room for all. An open area without trees, not far from water, is a perfect site for a Purple Martin house. In return for the lodging, the birds will feast on mosquitoes and other noxious insects.

Birds Attracted to Nest Boxes and Other Man-made Structures

American Kestrel (Sparrow Hawk)	Great Crested Flycatcher
American Robin	House Finch
Barn Owl	House Wren
Barn Swallow	Mourning Dove
Black-capped Chickadee	Northern Flicker
Brown Creeper	Osprey
Carolina Wren	Prothonotary Warbler
Chimney Swift	Purple Martin
Cliff Swallow	Ruby-throated Hummingbird
Common Nighthawk	Saw-whet Owl
Downy Woodpecker	Tree Swallow
Eastern Bluebird	Tufted Titmouse
Eastern Phoebe	White-breasted Nuthatch
Eastern Screech-Owl	Wood Duck

Shrubs and Trees

Landscaping for food and shelter is a necessity for a successful feeding station. Geographic location and local climate will influence the selection of plants. The planting of shrubs and trees may seem an overwhelming task, but nature will help if given a chance. Frequently, seedlings will pop up among bushes from a stray seed or from bird droppings.

Deciduous and evergreen shrubs, trees, and vines should be planted for their buds, fruits, or seeds. Several desirable species are listed below. Avoid non-native invasive plants.

Many deciduous trees are easy to plant, and in early spring they produce buds, flowers, and foliage that attract insect-eating birds. Alders, birches, and poplars also produce catkins, which provide seeds for later consumption. Cherry trees can be transplanted from the wild or might just appear from a stray seed dropped by a bird.

Aside from organized gardening, there are a number of miscellaneous suggestions that might be helpful. Thick, unrestrained shrubbery will provide good cover, as well as nesting and roosting sites. A discarded Christmas tree set up in the yard makes a good windbreak. A small dead (bare) tree, propped up, may become a favorite perch for resident birds. A wild corner given over to bittersweet, catbrier, chokeberry, and pokeberry will become an impenetrable tangle appealing to nesting Gray Catbirds or Northern Mockingbirds. If a utility wire runs through your property, watch it for perching flycatchers or migrating swallows. A well-trimmed lawn attracts American Robins and ant-pursuing Northern Flickers. The base of a privet hedge adjacent to an open lawn may be preferred by Ovenbirds, thrushes, sparrows, and even Indigo Buntings.

Some Deciduous and Evergreen Trees, Shrubs, and Vines That Should Be Planted for Their Buds, Fruits, or Seeds

Alder	Birch
Arborvitae (Northern White Cedar)	Bittersweet
Ash	Blackberry
Atlantic White Cedar	Blueberry
Aspen	Box Elder
Bayberry	Buttonbush
Beech	Catbrier

Cherry
Chokeberry
Cottonwood
Crab Apple
Currant
Dogwood
Elderberry
Fir
Firebush
Grape (Wild)
Hackberry
Hawthorn
Hemlock
Hercules Club
Holly
Huckleberry
Maple
Mountain Ash
Mulberry
Oak
Pecan

Persimmon
Pine
Pokeberry
Poplar
Privet
Quince (Flowering)
Raspberry
Red Cedar
Rhododendron(s)
Sassafras
Shadbush
Sour Gum (Tupelo)
Spicebush
Spruce
Sumac
Sweet Gum
Tulip Tree
Viburnum
Walnut
Yew

Appendix A: Optical Equipment

Whether at home or away, one can watch birds with the naked eye, but to identify them correctly and to study them well some optical equipment is essential. At first, perhaps, 2- or 3-power opera glasses might be sufficient, but in order to bring a bird up close enough to observe fine details, a pair of prism binoculars is a must.

Start with a lightweight pair, the magnification of which should be no more than 7 to 8 power; that is, the bird under observation should appear at least seven times closer than if viewed without binoculars. Binoculars that are either 7 X 35, or, even better, 7 X 50 are undoubtedly the best. Binoculars more powerful than 7 or 8 will be heavier and more cumbersome to use. Remember—the figure after the X represents the amount of light; 50 is better than 35.

Be certain that the binoculars you buy have a central focus, that is, a wheel or other device in the center to turn or focus both lenses quickly and at the same time. This feature is most important, especially for viewing moving birds, for which instant focusing is imperative.

When purchasing optical equipment, make sure that the lenses are clear and that no distortions are present. Do *not* buy binoculars until you have looked through them. They must be in perfect order in every respect, including proper alignment, so as not to strain your eyes. When the binoculars are not in use, keep them in their carrying case.

For those birds that are seen at a distance, such as waterfowl on the other side of a large lake or perhaps a hawk on a high cliff, something more powerful is needed. Especially useful is a telescope mounted on a tripod. The scope should range anywhere from 10 to 20 power and, preferably, should have a zoom lens for quick results. In telescopes of higher power, vibration and atmospheric interference can blur the image; therefore, anything stronger than 20 power is not recommended. Furthermore, the objective may be blurred because of heat haze or merely less light, causing less sharpness.

Also necessary is a lightweight tripod on which to mount the telescope. Be sure that the legs have clamps that press down to make them more secure. *Never* buy a tripod that has leg screws. Sand and grit will get into the threads, and constant loosening and tightening will cause the joints to become threadbare.

Appendix B: Glossary

Barred: crosswise *horizontal* markings, as in tails of many hawks

Breeding: spring, summer—periods or plumages

Decurved: downward curved bill

Facial disk: rounded front part of face, as in owls

Frontal shield: bare covering at the base of bill, as in gallinules

Head tuft: clump of feathers on top of head, as in owls and Horned Lark

Lobed: partially webbed

Lore: space between bill and eye

Mandibles: upper and lower bills

Median line: stripe through center of crown

Nape: back of neck

Nonbreeding: fall, winter—periods or plumages

Primaries: long flight feathers on outer wing

Rectrices: tail feathers

Rump: lower back just above tail

Secondaries: long flight feathers on inner wing

Semipalmated: partially webbed

Serrated: "toothed" bill edge, as in mergansers

Spectacle: eye ring, with connecting streak through lore

Streaked: lengthwise markings, as in many sparrows

Tarsus: the generally exposed "shin" part of leg

Vent: undertail feather groups

Vermiculated: fine, wavy, lateral streaks on feathers

Index

Anhinga *(Anhinga anhinga)*, 102
Avocet, American *(Recurvirostra americana)*, 114

Bittern, American *(Botaurus lentiginosus)*, 110
Bittern, Least *(Ixobrychus exilis)*, 110
Blackbird, Red-winged *(Agelaius phoeniceus)*, 30
Bluebird, Eastern *(Sialia sialis)*, 22
Bobolink *(Dolichonyx oryzivorus)*, 34
Bobwhite, Northern *(Colinus virginianus)*, 70
Brant *(Branta bernicla)*, 84
Bufflehead *(Bucephala albeola)*, 92
Bunting, Indigo *(Passerina cyanea)*, 22
Bunting, Painted *(Passerina ciris)*, 24
Bunting, Snow *(Plectrophenax nivalis)*, 34

Canvasback *(Aythya valisineria)*, 90
Cardinal, Northern *(Cardinalis cardinalis)*, 24
Catbird, Gray *(Dumetella carolinensis)*, 44
Chickadee, Black-capped *(Poecile atricapillus)*, 46
Coot, American *(Fulica americana)*, 96
Cormorant, Double-crested *(Phalacrocorax auritus)*, 102
Cormorant, Great *(Phalacrocorax carbo)*, 102
Cormorant, Neotropic (Olivaceous) *(Phalacrocorax brasilianus)*, 102
Cowbird, Brown-headed *(Molothrus ater)*, 30
Crane, Sandhill *(Grus canadensis)*, 108
Creeper, Brown *(Certhia americana)*, 58
Crow, American *(Corvus brachyrhynchos)*, 28
Cuckoo, Yellow-billed *(Coccyzus americanus)*, 68

Dickcissel *(Spiza americana)*, 40

Dove, Common Ground- *(Columbina passerina)*, 68
Dove, Mourning *(Zenaida macroura)*, 68
Dowitcher, Short-billed *(Limnodromus griseus)*, 118
Duck, American Black *(Anas rubripes)*, 86
Duck, Muscovy *(Cairina moschata)*, 86
Duck, Ring-necked *(Aythya collaris)*, 90
Duck, Ruddy *(Oxyura jamaicensis)*, 90
Duck, Wood *(Aix sponsa)*, 88
Dunlin *(Calidris alpina)*, 122

Eagle, Bald *(Haliaeetus leucocephalus)*, 72
Egret, Cattle *(Bubulcus ibis)*, 106
Egret, Great *(Ardea alba)*, 106
Egret, Reddish *(Egretta rufescens)*, 106, 108
Egret, Snowy *(Egretta thula)*, 106
Eider, Common *(Somateria mollissima)*, 94

Finch, House *(Carpodacus mexicanus)*, 26
Finch, Purple *(Carpodacus purpureus)*, 26
Flicker, Northern *(Colaptes auratus)*, 60
Flycatcher, Great Crested *(Myiarchus crinitus)*, 62
Flycatcher, Least *(Empidonax minimus)*, 62
Frigatebird, Magnificent *(Fregata magnificens)*, 104

Gadwall *(Anas strepera)*, 86
Gallinule, Purple *(Porphyrio martinica)*, 96
Gannet, Northern *(Morus bassanus)*, 104
Gnatcatcher, Blue-gray *(Polioptila caerulea)*, 46
Godwit, Marbled *(Limosa fedoa)*, 118
Goldeneye, Common *(Bucephala clangula)*, 92
Goldfinch, American *(Carduelis tristis)*, 32
Goose, Canada *(Branta canadensis)*, 84
Goose, Snow *(Chen caerulescens)*, 84
Grackle, Boat-tailed *(Quiscalus major)*, 28
Grackle, Common *(Quiscalus quiscula)*, 28

Grebe, Horned *(Podiceps auritus)*, 98
Grebe, Pied-billed *(Podilymbus podiceps)*, 98
Grebe, Red-necked *(Podiceps grisegena)*, 98
Grosbeak, Blue *(Passerina caerulea)*, 22
Grosbeak, Evening *(Coccothraustes vespertinus)*, 32
Grosbeak, Rose-breasted *(Pheucticus ludovicianus)*, 26
Ground-Dove, Common *(Columbina passerina)*, 68
Grouse, Ruffed *(Bonasa umbellus)*, 70
Guillemot, Black *(Cepphus grylle)*, 100
Gull, Bonaparte's *(Larus philadelphia)*, 124
Gull, Great Black-backed *(Larus marinus)*, 124
Gull, Herring *(Larus argentatus)*, 124
Gull, Laughing *(Larus atricilla)*, 124
Gull, Ring-billed *(Larus delawarensis)*, 124

Harrier, Northern (Marsh Hawk) *(Circus cyaneus)*, 74
Hawk, Broad-winged *(Buteo platypterus)*, 76
Hawk, Red-shouldered *(Buteo lineatus)*, 76
Hawk, Red-tailed *(Buteo jamaicensis)*, 76
Hawk, Rough-legged *(Buteo lagopus)*, 76
Hawk, Sharp-shinned *(Accipiter striatus)*, 78
Heron, Black-crowned Night- *(Nycticorax nycticorax)*, 110
Heron, Great Blue *(Ardea herodias)*, 108
Heron, "Great White" *(Ardea herodias)*, 106
Heron, Green *(Butorides virescens)*, 110
Heron, Little Blue *(Egretta caerulea)*, 106, 108
Heron, Tricolored (Louisiana) *(Egretta tricolor)*, 108
Heron, Yellow-crowned Night- *(Nyctanassa violacea)*, 110
Hummingbird, Ruby-throated *(Archilochus colubris)*, 66

Ibis, Glossy *(Plegadis falcinellus)*, 112
Ibis, White *(Eudocimus albus)*, 112

Jay, Blue *(Cyanocitta cristata)*, 22
Junco, Dark-eyed *(Junco hyemalis)*, 40

Kestrel, American (Sparrow Hawk) *(Falco sparverius)*, 78
Killdeer *(Charadrius vociferus)*, 116
Kingbird, Eastern *(Tyrannus tyrannus)*, 62
Kingbird, Gray *(Tyrannus dominicensis)*, 62
Kingfisher, Belted *(Ceryle alcyon)*, 22
Kinglet, Golden-crowned *(Regulus satrapa)*, 46
Kinglet, Ruby-crowned *(Regulus calendula)*, 46
Kite, Swallow-tailed *(Elanoides forficatus)*, 74
Knot, Red *(Calidris canutus)*, 122

Lark, Horned *(Eremophila alpestris)*, 34
Limpkin *(Aramus guarauna)*, 112
Loon, Common *(Gavia immer)*, 100
Loon, Red-throated *(Gavia stellata)*, 100

Mallard *(Anas platyrhynchos)*, 86
Martin, Purple *(Progne subis)*, 64
Meadowlark, Eastern *(Sturnella magna)*, 34
Merganser, Common *(Mergus merganser)*, 92
Merganser, Hooded *(Lophodytes cucullatus)*, 92
Merganser, Red-breasted *(Mergus serrator)*, 92
Merlin *(Falco columbarius)*, 78
Mockingbird, Northern *(Mimus polyglottos)*, 44
Moorhen, Common (Common Gallinule) *(Gallinula chloropus)*, 96

Night-Heron, Black-crowned *(Nycticorax nycticorax)*, 110
Night-Heron, Yellow-crowned *(Nyctanassa violacea)*, 110
Nighthawk, Common *(Chordeiles minor)*, 66
Nuthatch, Red-breasted *(Sitta canadensis)*, 58
Nuthatch, White-breasted *(Sita carolinensis)*, 58

Oldsquaw *(Clangula hyemalis)*, 94

Oriole, Baltimore (Northern) *(Icterus galbula)*, 32

Oriole, Orchard *(Icterus spurius)*, 32

Osprey *(Pandion haliaetus)*, 74

Ovenbird *(Seiurus aurocapilla)*, 38

Owl, Barn *(Tyto alba)*, 82

Owl, Barred *(Strix varia)*, 80

Owl, Burrowing *(Athene cunicularia)*, 82

Owl, Eastern Screech- *(Otus asio)*, 80

Owl, Great Horned *(Bubo virginianus)*, 80

Owl, Long-eared *(Asio otus)*, 80

Owl, Saw-whet *(Aegolius acadicus)*, 80

Owl, Short-eared *(Asio flammeus)*, 82

Owl, Snowy *(Nyctea scandiaca)*, 82

Oystercatcher, American *(Haematopus palliatus)*, 114

Pelican, Brown *(Pelecanus occidentalis)*, 104

Pelican, White *(Pelecanus erythrorhynchos)*, 104

Pewee, Eastern Wood- *(Contopus virens)*, 62

Pheasant, Ring-necked *(Phasianus colchicus)*, 70

Phoebe, Eastern *(Sayornis phoebe)*, 62

Pigeon, Rock (Dove) *(Columbia livia)*, 68

Pintail, Northern *(Anas acuta)*, 86

Pipit, American (Water) *(Anthus rubescens)*, 34

Plover, Black-bellied *(Pluvialis squatarola)*, 116

Plover, Piping *(Charadrius melodus)*, 116

Plover, Semipalmated *(Charadrius semipalmatus)*, 116

Rail, Clapper *(Rallus longirostris)*, 96

Rail, Virginia *(Rallus limicola)*, 96

Redhead *(Aytha americana)*, 90

Redpoll, Common *(Carduelis flammea)*, 26

Redstart, American *(Setophaga ruticilla)*, 56

Robin, American *(Turdus migratorius)*, 36

Sanderling *(Calidris alba)*, 122

Sandpiper, Least *(Calidris minutilla)*, 122

Sandpiper, Pectoral *(Calidris melanotos)*, 122

Sandpiper, Purple *(Calidris maritima)*, 122

Sandpiper, Semipalmated *(Calidris pusilla)*, 122

Sandpiper, Solitary *(Tringa solitaria)*, 120

Sandpiper, Spotted *(Actitis macularius)*, 120

Sandpiper, Upland *(Bartramia longicauda)*, 120

Sapsucker, Yellow-bellied *(Sphyrapicus varius)*, 60

Scaup, Greater *(Aythya marila)*, 90

Scaup, Lesser *(Aythya affinis)*, 90

Scoter, Black *(Melanitta nigra)*, 94

Scoter, Surf *(Melanitta perspicillata)*, 94

Scoter, White-winged *(Melanitta fusca)*, 94

Screech-Owl, Eastern *(Otus asio)*, 80

Shoveler, Northern *(Ana clypeata)*, 88

Shrike, Loggerhead *(Lanius ludovicianus)*, 44

Siskin, Pine *(Carduelis pinus)*, 32

Skimmer, Black *(Rynchops niger)*, 128

Snipe, Common *(Gallinago gallinago)*, 120

Sparrow, Chipping *(Spizella passerina)*, 42

Sparrow, Field *(Spizella pusilla)*, 42

Sparrow, Fox *(Passerella iliaca)*, 40

Sparrow, House *(Passer domesticus)*, 40

Sparrow, Savannah *(Passerculus sandwichensis)*, 40

Sparrow, Song *(Melospiza melodia)*, 40

Sparrow, Swamp *(Melospiza georgiana)*, 42

Sparrow, Tree *(Spizella arborea)*, 42

Sparrow, White-crowned *(Zonotrichia leucophrys)*, 42

Sparrow, White-throated *(Zonotrichia albicollis)*, 42

Spoonbill, Roseate *(Platalea ajaja)*, 112

Starling, European *(Sturnus vulgaris)*, 30

Stilt, Black-necked *(Himantopus mexicanus)*, 114

Stork, Wood *(Mycteria americana)*, 112

Swallow, Bank *(Riparia riparia)*, 64
Swallow, Barn *(Hirundo rustica)*, 64
Swallow, Cliff *(Petrochelidon pyrrhonota)*, 64
Swallow, Tree *(Tachycineta bicolor)*, 64
Swan, Mute *(Cygnus olor)*, 84
Swan, Tundra (Whistling) *(Cygnus columbianus)*, 84
Swift, Chimney *(Chaetura pelagica)*, 64

Tanager, Scarlet *(Piranga olivacea)*, 24
Tanager, Summer *(Piranga rubra)*, 24
Teal, Blue-winged *(Anas discors)*, 88
Teal, Green-winged *(Anas crecca)*, 88
Tern, Black *(Chlidonias niger)*, 126
Tern, Caspian *(Sterna caspia)*, 128
Tern, Common *(Sterna hirundo)*, 126
Tern, Gull-billed *(Sterna nilotica)*, 126
Tern, Least *(Sterna antillarum)*, 126
Tern, Royal *(Sterna maxima)*, 128
Tern, Sandwich *(Sterna sandvicensis)*, 128
Thrasher, Brown *(Toxostoma rufum)*, 38
Thrush, Hermit *(Catharus guttatus)*, 38
Thrush, Wood *(Hylocichla mustelina)*, 38
Titmouse, Tufted *(Baeolophus bicolor)*, 46
Towhee, Eastern (Rufous-sided) *(Pipilo erythrophthalmus)*, 36
Turkey, Wild *(Meleagris gallopavo)*, 70
Turnstone, Ruddy *(Arenaria interpres)*, 116

Vireo, Blue-headed (Solitary) *(Vireo solitarius)*, 48
Vireo, Red-eyed *(Vireo olivaceus)*, 48
Vireo, Warbling *(Vireo gilvus)*, 48
Vireo, White-eyed *(Vireo griseus)*, 48
Vireo, Yellow-throated *(Vireo flavifrons)*, 48
Vulture, Black *(Coragyps atratus)*, 72
Vulture, Turkey *(Cathartes aura)*, 72

Warbler, Bay-breasted *(Dendroica castanea)*, 56
Warbler, Black-and-White *(Mniotilta varia)*, 58
Warbler, Blackburnian *(Dendroica fusca)*, 56
Warbler, Blackpoll *(Dendroica striata)*, 54

Warbler, Black-throated Blue *(Dendroica caerulescens)*, 54
Warbler, Black-throated Green *(Dendroica virens)*, 54
Warbler, Blue-winged *(Vermivora pinus)*, 50
Warbler, Canada *(Wilsonia canadensis)*, 52
Warbler, Cape May *(Dendroica tigrina)*, 52
Warbler, Chestnut-sided *(Dendroica pensylvanica)*, 56
Warbler, Golden-winged *(Vermivora chrysoptera)*, 54
Warbler, Hooded *(Wilsonia citrina)*, 50
Warbler, Magnolia *(Dendroica magnolia)*, 52
Warbler, Nashville *(Vermivora ruficapilla)*, 50
Warbler, Northern Parula *(Parula americana)*, 56
Warbler, Palm *(Dendroica palmarum)*, 52
Warbler, Pine *(Dendroica pinus)*, 52
Warbler, Prairie *(Dendroica discolor)*, 52
Warbler, Prothonotary *(Protonotaria citrea)*, 50
Warbler, Wilson's *(Wilsonia pusilla)*, 50
Warbler, Yellow *(Dendroica petechia)*, 52
Warbler, Yellow-rumped (Myrtle) *(Dendroica coronata)*, 54
Warbler, Yellow-throated *(Dendroica dominica)*, 54
Waterthrush, Northern *(Seiurus noveboracensis)*, 38
Waxwing, Cedar *(Bombycilla cedrorum)*, 44
Whimbrel *(Numenius phaeopus)*, 118
Whip-poor-will *(Caprimulgus vociferus)*, 66
Wigeon, American (Baldpate) *(Anas americana)*, 88
Willet *(Catoptrophorus semipalmatus)*, 118
Woodcock, American *(Scolopax minor)*, 120
Woodpecker, Downy *(Picoides pubescens)*, 58
Woodpecker, Hairy *(Picoides villosus)*, 58
Woodpecker, Pileated *(Dryocopus pileatus)*, 60

Woodpecker, Red-bellied *(Melanerpes carolinus)*, 60

Woodpecker, Red-headed *(Melanerpes erythrocephalus)*, 60

Wood-Pewee, Eastern *(Contopus virens)*, 62

Wren, Carolina *(Thryothorus ludovicianus)*, 36

Wren, House *(Troglodytes aedon)*, 36

Wren, Marsh *(Cistothorus palustris)*, 36

Yellowlegs, Greater *(Tringa melanoleuca)*, 118

Yellowthroat, Common *(Geothlypis trichas)*, 50

About the Authors and Artist

John Bull, a leading authority on birds, was on the staff of the Ornithology Department of the American Museum of Natural History in New York City for many years. He is the author of two classics on Eastern birds—*Birds of the New York Area* (1964) and *Birds of New York State* (1974)—co-author of the best-selling *National Audubon Society Field Guide to North American Birds: Eastern Region* (1977), and has written numerous magazine and newspaper articles. He has served as a nature guide on tours around the world, is a familiar figure to birders in many area of the East, and has been a member of many ornithological associations.

Edith Bull majored in zoology at Skidmore College and received an M.A. in vertebrate paleontology from Columbia University. She worked in the Department of Vertebrate Paleontology at the American Museum of Natural History and conducted classes for children at the museum.

Gerald Gold was an editor, reporter, and columnist at the *New York Times* for forty-one years, until his retirement in 1991. He served as deputy foreign editor, deputy culture editor, magazine editor, consumer affairs columnist, and music editor. He was editor of the *Times's* publication of the Pentagon Papers in 1971, for which the paper won the Pulitzer Prize. The author of *Gandhi: A Pictorial Biography* (1983), with illustrations from the movie *Gandhi,* he is a long-time birder.

Pieter D. Prall, a New Jersey nature artist, helped edit this guide and its companion volume, *The Easy Bird Guide: Western Region.* A graduate of the School of Visual Arts in New York, he has been a volunteer technician in the Department of Ornithology at the American Museum of Natural History in New York and an Artist in Residence at the New Jersey Audubon Society. He was a founder of the Highlands Conservation Initiative, which led to the preservation of land in New York and New Jersey. His nature art has been published in *A Guide to the Birds of Colombia, American Birds* magazine, the *New York Times,* and the *Wall Street Journal.* His work has been shown at galleries, museums, and campuses in the United States, Canada, and Europe.